The Ethics of
Genetic Engineering

The Ethics of
Genetic Engineering

Other books in the At Issue series:

The Ethics of
Genetic Engineering

Maurya Siedler, *Book Editor*

Bruce Glassman, *Vice President*
Bonnie Szumski, *Publisher*
Helen Cothran, *Managing Editor*

GREENHAVEN PRESS
An imprint of Thomson Gale, a part of The Thomson Corporation

Detroit • New York • San Francisco • San Diego • New Haven, Conn.
Waterville, Maine • London • Munich

Thomson and Star Logo are trademarks and Gale and Greenhaven Press are registered trademarks used herein under license.

For more information, contact
Greenhaven Press
27500 Drake Rd.
Farmington Hills, MI 48331-3535
Or you can visit our Internet site at http://www.gale.com

LIBRARY OF CONGRESS CATALOGING-IN-PUBLICATION DATA

The ethics of genetic engineering / Maurya Siedler, book editor.
    p. cm. — (At issue)
Includes bibliographical references and index.
ISBN 0-7377-2370-X (lib. : alk. paper) — ISBN 0-7377-2371-8 (pbk. : alk. paper)
    1. Genetic engineering—Moral and ethical aspects. I. Siedler, Maurya.
II. At issue (San Diego, Calif.)
QH438.7.E842 2005
174'.966—dc22   2004042517

Printed in the United States of America

Contents

Introduction

Genetic engineering is the selective manipulation of an organism's genes by technological intervention. This technology enables scientists to change the genetic makeup of plants and animals, creating organisms with desired attributes and eliminating unwanted traits. By transferring genes from one species to another, it is possible to create entirely new organisms that do not occur naturally.

The potential benefits of genetic engineering are vast. They include the prevention and cure of disease, elimination of global food shortages, improvements in agriculture and eradication of industrial toxins. Many supporters of genetic research believe it is society's moral duty to pursue advancements that have such positive implications for humanity.

Despite its potential benefits, however, genetic engineering raises many moral issues that are not easily resolved. Some people believe that to manipulate the genetic codes is to assume power that belongs to God, not humans. Others argue that humans are gifted with the unique ability to think and reason, and should therefore use these powers to improve their health and lives. People also disagree about the possible environmental and social consequences of genetic engineering. One extremely controversial area of genetic engineering is research on human embryos.

Embryonic stem cell research

Embryonic stem cells are undifferentiated cells that have the potential to develop into any of the 220 types of cells in the body, such as bone cells, muscle cells, and blood cells. Scientists are trying to harvest these stem cells before they differentiate, and then coax them into becoming various cell types in the laboratory. They hope that they can use these cells to repair or replace damaged cells in people's bodies. For example, if they could grow nerve cells, they might be able to replace brain cells damaged by Parkinson's or Alzheimer's. Although no cures have been developed from stem cell research so far, researchers say the field is promising. Until recently, all of the research was conducted on embryos left over from fertility treatments or from abortions.

Opponents of stem cell research believe it is wrong because harvesting stem cells destroys the embryo, a potential human life. Many people object to the use of human embryos on religious grounds and question the kind of society that would use potential life as a resource for scientific research, even for the purpose of curing disease. In his remarks on stem cell research, President Bush noted, "There's no such thing as excess life, and the fact that a living being is going to die does not justify experimenting on it or exploiting it as a natural resource."

Critics of embryonic stem cell research also argue that instead of using embryos, scientists should carry out their research on adult stem cells and other cell sources. As an editorial in the *Western Catholic Reporter* states, "Our hope should be that other sources of stem cells—from adults . . . and from umbilical cords of newborns and placentas—will provide cures for many diseases. These sources of stem cells may provide life and health without also destroying life."

Advocates of stem cell research argue that aborted fetuses and embryos discarded by fertility clinics are destined to be destroyed anyway and should be put to use in research for the greater good of humanity, ultimately saving lives. They believe that the stem cells from embryos offer a greater promise for curing disease and alleviating suffering than adult cells, which they say are not as flexible as embryonic cells and are therefore less capable of growing into different kinds of tissue. Many celebrities such as actors Michael J. Fox and Christopher Reeve and former first lady Nancy Reagan have made impassioned pleas to allow federal funding of stem cell research to bring an end to catastrophic diseases and conditions. At congressional hearings in 2000, Reeve asked, "Is it more ethical for a woman to donate unused embryos that will never become human beings, or let them be tossed away as so much garbage when they could help save thousands of lives?"

Therapeutic cloning

In the past few years, the debate over embryonic stem cell research has become even more complex because of the successful cloning of human embryos. In 2001 the Massachusetts-based company Advanced Cell Technology announced that it had cloned embryos by implanting DNA from an adult human into an egg cell, which was then stimulated to grow into a six-cell, early stage embryo, called a blastocyst. As a result, another controversial source of embryos for stem cell research is now available, raising more fears and hopes. Some people believe that cloning embryos for research purposes will lead to the commercialization and cheapening of human life. They envision a world in which human embryos will be coldly viewed as the raw material for medical products. Eventually biotech companies might seek greater profits by using embryo research to produce "enhancement" medicine rather than cures for serious diseases. As law professor Lori B. Andrews describes, "Where cardiac patients might need new heart cells to repair a damaged chamber, athletes may use these same cells to increase stamina." On the other hand, supporters of therapeutic cloning argue that it is not immoral to experiment on cloned blastocysts because they consist of only a few cells, cannot feel, and therefore cannot be categorized as human beings. They believe that the research results will be used for the greater good of society.

The importance of public awareness

Researchers continue to expand the limits of genetic engineering, and it is clear that this science is an inevitable part of the future world. However, these rapid advances are outpacing the development of laws to regulate them, leaving many people feeling concerned that society is charging down a dangerous path without a full consideration of the consequences. Both opponents and advocates of genetic engineering believe that the public needs to develop a greater awareness of this new and relatively unfamiliar science in order to engage in educated debates and make informed choices. As genetic engineering critic Jeremy Rifkin points out, "It is up to the public and the next generation in particular to politicize and argue, challenge and express their views in the streets, in the courts, the media, and so on." In *At Issue: The Ethics of Genetic Engineering*, the authors offer a variety of perspectives on many aspects of this extremely controversial subject.

1

An Overview of the Ethical Debates in Genetic Engineering

Desmond S.T. Nicholl

Desmond S.T. Nicholl is a senior lecturer and associate dean of faculty in the department of biological sciences at the University of Paisley in Scotland. He is the author of An Introduction to Genetic Engineering.

Science is not morally neutral because its applications pose many ethical dilemmas, particularly in the field of genetic engineering. These include genetic screening for predisposition to disease, gene patenting, xenotransplantation (transplanting animal organs into humans), genetically modified foods, human cloning, and transgenic organisms (transferring genes between species). Scientists who develop new genetic technologies usually act with the highest integrity. However, when commercial interests become involved, responsibility and accountability sometimes deteriorate.

I t is often said that science *per se* is neither 'good' nor 'bad', and that it is therefore ethically and morally neutral. Whilst this may be true of science as a *process*, it is the developments and applications that arise from the scientific process that pose the ethical questions. The example that is often quoted is the development of the atomic bomb—the science was interesting and novel, and of itself ethically neutral, but the application (i.e. use of the devices in conflict) posed a completely different set of moral and ethical questions. Also, science is, of course,

Desmond S.T. Nicholl, *An Introduction to Genetic Engineering*. New York: Cambridge University Press, 2002. Copyright © 2002 by Cambridge University Press. Reproduced by permission.

11

carried out by *scientists*, who are most definitely not ethically and morally neutral, as they demonstrate the same breadth and range of opinion as the rest of the human race. An assumption often made by the layman is that scientists and the scientific process are the same thing, which is unfortunate.

Despite the purist argument that science is in some way immune from ethical considerations, I believe that to separate the process from its applications is an artificial distinction. In the developed world we live in societies shaped by technology, which is derived from the application of scientific discoveries. We must all share the responsibility of policing the new genetic technology.

The various ethical dilemmas

Advances in the basic science of genetics usually pose few problems from an ethical standpoint. The major concerns are usually separate from the actual experiments—perhaps the use of animals in research, or the potential for transgenic crops to contaminate non-transgenic or wild populations. We will consider some of the ethical problems in medicine, biotechnology, transgenic organisms, and organismal cloning. . . . However, there is considerable overlap in many of these areas, and it is again somewhat artificial to separate these topics.

> *The apparent arrogance of biotechnology companies upsets people who might actually agree with the overall aims of the company.*

In medicine, few would argue against the development of new drugs and therapies, where clear benefit is obtained. Perhaps the one area in the medically related applications of genetic research that is difficult is the human genome information. Genetic screening, and thus the possibility of genetic discrimination, is an area of active debate at the moment. The molecular diagnosis of genetically based disease is now well established, and the major ethical dilemmas tend to centre around whether or not a foetus should be aborted if a disease-causing trait is detected. If and when it becomes possible to screen routinely for polygenic and multifactorial traits, perhaps involving personality and predisposition to behavioural problems, the ethical picture will become even more complex. This whole area of predisposition, as opposed to a confirmed causal link between genes and disease, is a difficult area in which to establish any ethical rules, as many of the potential problems are as yet hypothetical.

The biotechnology industry is a difficult area to define, as the applications of gene technology in biotech applications are very diverse. The one ethical thread linking disparate applications is the influence of commercial interests. Patenting gene sequences raises questions, as does the production of products such as bovine somatotropin (BST). Many people see biotechnology applications as driven by commercial pressures, and some are uneasy with this. Similar questions can be asked of any manufacturing process, but the use of biological material seems to set up a different attitude in many people. In some cases the apparent arrogance of biotechnology companies upsets people who might actually agree with the overall aims of the company, and several biotech companies have found that this public opinion can be a potent force in determining the success or failure of a product.

Transgenic plants and animals

Transgenic organisms set up several ethical questions. The one thing that has been a little surprising is the reversal of the usual plant/animal debate as far as transgenesis is concerned. Traditionally, animal welfare has been the major source of difficulty between pressure groups, concerned individuals, scientists and regulators. Plants were largely ignored in the ethical debate until the late 1990s, when the public backlash against genetically modified foods began to influence what biotech companies were doing. Concerns were in two areas—the effect of GMO [genetically modified organism]–derived foods on health, and the effect on the environment. The environmental debate in particular has been driven by many different groups, who claim that an ecological disaster might be waiting to emerge from GM [genetically modified] plant technology due to cross-pollination. It is impossible to predict what might happen in such cases, although the protagonists of GM crops claim to have evaluated the risks. The simple answer is that we do not know what the long-term ecological effects might be.

Transgenic animals have not posed as big a problem as plants.

This is a little surprising, but can be explained by the fact that animals are much easier to identify and contain (they need to copulate rather than pollinate!) and therefore any risk of transgenic traits getting into wild populations is much lower than for crop plants. Also, transgenic animals are often used in a medical context, where the benefits are obvious and generally appreciated. Welfare issues are still a concern, but the standard of care for animals in transgenic research is very high, and tightly monitored in most countries. Overall the acceptance of transgenic mouse models for disease, and transgenic animals as bioreactors, seems to pose less of a problem generally than aspects of plant biotechnology. The possibility of xenotransplantation,[1] offers hope but also raises questions, particularly for groups with specific religious objections to this type of application.

> *The responsibility for using genetic technology lies with those who discover, adapt, implement and regulate it.*

Organismal cloning is perhaps the most difficult area from an ethical viewpoint, as the possibility of human cloning exists and is being taken seriously by some. There is debate about the unique nature of personality, character, soul, nature or whatever it might be called; what would a cloned individual actually *be*? Views range from those who think that he or she would be in some sort of limbo, to those who see essentially no difference between a clone and a normal individual.

In a similar way to the progression of the Dolly research [cloned sheep], and its extension into transgenic cloning (Polly), many people fear that the possibility of generating transgenic 'designer babies' may become reality at some point in the future. Normal conception, genetic screening, transgenesis to replace defective genes, implantation and development to full term? Or perhaps selection of a set of characteristics from a list, and production of the desired phenotype by manipulating the genome? This all sounds very fanciful at present, even absurd. In the early 1990s informed opinion said the same thing about cloning from adult cells. Dolly arrived in 1996. . . .

---

1. the use of tissues or organs from a nonhuman source for transplantations

The responsibility of genetic technology

In trying to answer the question 'is it good or bad', we have seen that there can be no answer to this. As with any branch of human activity, the responsibility for using genetic technology lies with those who discover, adapt, implement and regulate it. However, the pressures that exist when commercial development of genetic engineering is undertaken can sometimes change the balance of responsibility. Most scientists ply their trade with honesty and integrity, and would not dream of falsifying results or inventing data. They take a special pride in what they do, and in a curious paradox remain detached from it, whilst being totally involved with it. Once the science becomes a technology, things are not quite so clear cut, and corporate responsibility is sometimes not quite so easy to define as individual responsibility.

2

Genetic Engineering Has Many Benefits for Society

Biotechnology Industry Organization

Formed in 1993, Biotechnology Industry Organization (BIO) represents biotechnology companies, academic institutions, state biotechnology centers, and related organizations that support the use of biotechnology in agriculture, health care, and other fields. BIO works to educate the public about biotechnology and responds to concerns about the safety and ethics of genetic engineering. The organization has members from over forty-four nations.

The field of genetic engineering is still in its infancy but is already promising many valuable health care applications for the diagnosis, treatment, and prevention of diseases. Genetic engineers are developing tests that can identify patients with a propensity for a particular disease and give them the chance to take measures to avoid getting sick. They are also creating tests that allow diseases to be diagnosed in their early stages, thereby improving the prognosis for patients. Another benefit of genetic engineering is the development of gene therapies to treat diseases such as cancer, chronic heart failure, and diabetes. Although biotechnology has already greatly improved health care, future advances in genetic research and product development will revolutionize the practice of medicine.

B iotechnology tools and techniques open new research avenues for discovering how healthy bodies work and what goes wrong when problems arise. Knowing the molecular basis of health and disease leads to improved and novel methods for treating and preventing diseases. In human health care, biotechnology products include quicker and more accurate diagnostic tests, therapies with fewer side effects because they are based on the body's self-healing capabilities, and new and safer vaccines. . . .

The wealth of genomics information made available by the Human Genome Project[1] will greatly assist doctors in early diagnosis of hereditary diseases, such as type I diabetes, cystic fibrosis, early-onset Alzheimer's and Parkinson's disease, that previously were detectable only after clinical symptoms appeared. Genetic tests will also identify patients with a propensity to diseases, such as various cancers, osteoporosis, emphysema, type II diabetes and asthma, giving patients an opportunity to prevent the disease by avoiding the triggers, such as diet, smoking and other environmental factors. . . .

Genetic engineering uses natural products as therapeutics

Many living organisms produce compounds that coincidentally have therapeutic value for us. For example, most antibiotics are produced by microbes, and a number of medicines on the market, such as digitalis, are plant products. Plant cell culture, recombinant DNA [deoxyribonucleic acid] technology and cellular cloning, now provide us with new ways to tap into natural diversity. As a result, we are investigating many plants and animals as sources of new medicines. Ticks could provide anticoagulants, and poison-arrow frogs might be a source of new painkillers. A fungus produces a novel, antioxidant enzyme that is particularly efficient at mopping up free radicals known to encourage tumor growth.

The ocean presents a particularly rich habitat for potential new medicines. Marine biotechnologists have discovered organisms containing compounds that could heal wounds, destroy tumors, prevent inflammation, relieve pain and kill microorganisms. Shells from marine crustaceans, such as shrimp and crabs, are made of chitin, a carbohydrate that is proving to be an effective drug-delivery vehicle. . . .

Gene therapy is a promising technology that uses genes, or related molecules such as RNA [ribonucleic acid] to treat dis-

1. a national research project to identify and sequence the genes in human DNA

eases. For example, rather than giving daily injections of missing proteins, physicians could supply the patient's body with an accurate instruction manual—a nondefective gene—correcting the genetic defect so the body itself makes the proteins. Other genetic diseases could be treated by using small pieces of RNA to block mutated genes.

Only certain genetic diseases are amenable to correction via replacement gene therapy. These are diseases caused by the lack of a protein, such as hemophilia and severe combined immunodeficiency disease (SCID), commonly known as the "bubble boy disease." Some children with SCID are being treated with gene therapy and enjoying relatively normal lives. Hereditary disorders that can be traced to the production of a defective protein, such as Huntington's disease, are best treated with RNA that interferes with protein production.

Medical researchers have also discovered that gene therapy can treat diseases other than hereditary genetic disorders. They have used briefly introduced genes, or transient gene therapy, as therapeutics for a variety of cancers, autoimmune disease, chronic heart failure, disorders of the nervous system and AIDS.

Cell transplants

Approximately 10 people die each day waiting for organs to become available for transplantation. To circumvent this problem, scientists are investigating how to use cell culture to increase the number of patients who might benefit from one organ donor. Liver cells grown in culture and implanted into patients kept them alive until a liver became available. To treat type 1 diabetes, researchers implanted insulin-producing cells from organ donors into the subjects' livers. Eighty percent of the patients required no insulin injections one year after receiving pancreatic cells; after two years, 71 percent had no need for insulin injections, in another study, skeletal muscle cells from the subject repaired damage to cardiac muscle caused by a heart attack.

As is true of patients receiving whole-organ transplant, expensive drugs for suppressing the immune response must be given if the transplanted cells are from someone other than the patient. Researchers are devising ways to keep the immune system from attacking the new cells. Cell encapsulation allows cells to secrete hormones or provide a specific metabolic function without being recognized by the immune system. As such, they can be implanted without rejection. Other researchers are genetically engineering cells to express a naturally occurring protein that disables immune system cells that bind to it.

Other conditions that could potentially be treated with cell transplants are cirrhosis, epilepsy and Parkinson's disease.

The functions of our immune system

We are using biotechnology to enlist the help of our immune systems in fighting a variety of diseases. Like the armed forces that defend countries, the immune system is made up of different branches, each containing different types of "soldiers" that interact with each other and the role players in other branches in complex, multifaceted ways.

For example, the cytokine branch stimulates other immune system branches and includes the interleukins, interferons and colony-stimulating factors, all of which are proteins. Because of biotechnology, they can now be produced in sufficient quantities to be marketed as therapeutics. Small doses of interleukin-2 have been effective in treating various cancers and AIDS, while interleukin-12 has shown promise in treating infectious diseases such as malaria and tuberculosis.

Researchers can also increase the number of a specific type of cell, with a highly specific function, from the cellular branch of the immune system. Under certain conditions, the immune system may not produce enough of the cell type a patient needs. Cell culture and natural growth factors that stimulate cell division allow researchers to shift the cellular balance toward the needed cell type.

> *In the United States more than 60,000 people are on organ recipient lists, while another 100,000 need organs, but are not on lists.*

Cancer vaccines that help the immune system find and kill tumors have also shown therapeutic potential. Unlike other vaccines, cancer vaccines are given after the patient has contracted the disease, so they are not preventative. They work by intensifying the reactions between the immune system and tumor.

In organ-transplant rejections and autoimmune diseases,

suppressing our immune system is in our best interest. Currently we are using monoclonal antibodies [derived from a single cell] to suppress, very selectively, the type of cell in the immune system responsible for organ-transplant rejection and autoimmune diseases, such as rheumatoid arthritis and multiple sclerosis. Patients given the biotechnology-based therapeutic show significantly less transplant rejection than those given cyclosporin, a medicine that suppresses all immune function and leaves organ-transplant patients vulnerable to infection.

Inflammation, another potentially destructive immune system response, can cause diseases characterized by chronic inflammation, such as ulcerative colitis. . . . A number of biotechnology companies are investigating therapeutic compounds that block the actions or decrease production of these cytokines.

The promise of xenotransplantation

Organ transplantation provides an especially effective, cost-efficient treatment for severe, life-threatening diseases of the heart, kidney and other organs. According to the United Network of Organ Sharing (UNOS), in the United States more than 60,000 people are on organ recipient lists, while another 100,000 need organs, but are not on lists.

Organs and cells from other species—pigs and other animals—may be promising sources of donor organs and therapeutic cells. This concept is called xenotransplantation.

The most significant obstacle to xenotransplantation is the immune system's self-protective response. When nonhuman tissue is introduced into the body, the body cuts off blood flow to the donated organ. The most promising method for overcoming this rejection may be various types of genetic modification. One approach deletes the pig gene for the enzyme that is the main cause of rejection; another adds human genetic material to disguise the pig cells as human cells.

The potential spread of infectious disease from other species to humans through xenotransplantation needs close attention. However, a 1999 study of 160 people who had received pig cells as part of treatments showed no signs of ill health related to this exposure. In addition, scientists have recently succeeded at deleting the gene that triggers immune activity from a type of pig that cannot be infected with the virus that causes the most concern.

Tissue engineering

Biotechnology permits the use of the human body's natural capacity to repair and maintain itself. The body's toolbox for self-repair and maintenance includes many different proteins and various populations of stem cells that have the capacity to cure diseases, repair injuries and reverse age-related wear and tear.

Tissue engineering combines advances in cell biology and materials science, allowing us to create semi-synthetic tissues and organs in the lab. These tissues consist of biocompatible scaffolding material, which eventually degrades and is absorbed, plus living cells grown using cell culture techniques. Ultimately the goal is to create whole organs consisting of different tissue types to replace diseased or injured organs.

The most basic forms of tissue engineering use natural biological materials, such as collagen, for scaffolding. For example, two-layer skin is made by infiltrating a collagen gel with connective tissue cells, then creating the outer skin with a layer of tougher protective cells. In other methods, rigid scaffolding, made of a synthetic polymer, is shaped and then placed in the body where new tissue is needed. Other synthetic polymers, made from natural compounds, create flexible scaffolding more appropriate for soft-tissue structures, like blood vessels and bladders. When the scaffolding is placed in the body, adjacent cells invade it. At other times, the biodegradable implant is spiked with cells grown in the laboratory prior to implantation.

> *Stem cell therapies could revolutionize approaches for treating many of our most deadly and debilitating diseases.*

Simple tissues, such as skin and cartilage, were the first to be engineered successfully. Recently, however, physicians have achieved remarkable results with a biohybrid kidney that maintains patients with acute renal failure until the injured kidney repairs itself. A group of patients with only a 10 to 20 percent probability of survival regained normal kidney function and left the hospital in good health because the hybrid kidney prevented the events that typically follow kidney failure: infection, sepsis and multi-organ failure. The hybrid kidney is made of hollow tubes seeded with kidney stem cells that proliferate until they line the tube's inner wall. These cells develop into the type of kidney cell that releases hormones and is involved with filtration and transportation. In addition to carrying out these expected metabolic functions, the cells in the hybrid kidney also responded to signals produced by the patient's other organs and tissues.

Therapeutic proteins produced by transgenic animals

The human body produces an array of small proteins known as growth factors that promote cell growth, stimulate cell division and, in some cases, guide cell differentiation. These proteins can be used to help wounds heal, regenerate injured tissue and advance the development of tissue engineering described earlier. As proteins they are prime candidates for large-scale production by transgenic organisms [containing genes from different species], which would enable their use as therapeutic agents.

Some of the most common growth factors are epidermal growth factor, which stimulates skin cell division and could be used to encourage wound healing; erythropoietin, which stimulates the formation of red blood cells and was one of the first biotechnology products; fibroblast growth factor, which stimulates cell growth and has been effective in healing burns, ulcers and bone and growing new blood vessels in patients with blocked coronary arteries; transforming growth factor-beta, which helps fetal cells differentiate into different tissue types and triggers the formation of new tissue in adults; and nerve growth factors, which encourage nerve cells to grow, repair damage and could be used in patients with head and spinal cord injuries or degenerative diseases such as Alzheimer's.

Stem cells could revolutionize medicine

Stem cell research represents the cutting edge of science—a biotechnology method that uses cell culture techniques to grow and maintain stable cell lines. Stem cell therapies could revolutionize approaches for treating many of our most deadly and debilitating diseases and afflictions such as diabetes, Parkinson's, Alzheimer's, stroke and spinal cord injuries. Development of the remarkable biohybrid kidney described above depended on a supply of kidney stem cells. Doctors used blood stem cells to repair the damaged heart of a 16-year-old boy who had suffered a heart attack following an accident that punctured his heart. They harvested stem cells from his blood, rather than extracting them from bone marrow, and injected them into the coronary arteries that supply blood to the heart muscle.

Most cells in the human body are differentiated—meaning they have a specific shape, size and function. Some cells exist only to carry oxygen through the bloodstream, others to transmit nerve signals to the brain and so forth. Stem cells are cells that have not yet differentiated. Different types of stem cells display varying degrees of plasticity regarding their potential fate.

In adults, some tissues maintain a population of stem cells to replenish cells that have died or been injured; other tissues have no resident stem cell populations. When an adult stem cell receives a cue to differentiate, it first divides in two: One daughter cell differentiates, the other remains undifferentiated, ensuring a continual supply of stem cells. Bone marrow contains stem cells that can differentiate into any of the cell types found in blood, such as red blood cells, T-cells and lymphocytes, and bone. Liver stem cells can become any of the specialized cells of the liver—bile-secreting cells, storage cells or cells that line the bile duct. But stem cells in the liver do not differentiate into T-cells, and bone marrow stem cells do not become liver cells.

> *Researchers are developing vaccines against diseases such as diabetes, chronic inflammatory disease, Alzheimer's disease and cancers.*

In 1998, researchers reported that they had established human embryonic stem lines. This breakthrough opened up many avenues for treating diseases and healing injured tissue because embryonic stem cells can become any kind of cell in the body. Embryonic stem cells are derived from a blastocyst, which is the ball of about 150 undifferentiated cells from which an embryo develops. In addition to their total developmental plasticity, embryonic stem cells can produce more of themselves without limit.

By starting with undifferentiated adult and embryonic stem cells, scientists may be able to grow cells to replace tissue damaged from heart disease, spinal cord injuries and burns, and to treat diseases such as Parkinson's, diabetes and Alzheimer's by replacing malfunctioning cells with newly differentiated healthy cells. This process of culturing a line of genetically identical cells to replace defective cells in the body is sometimes referred to as therapeutic cloning.

Creating genetically identical cells

The potential value of stem cell therapy and tissue engineering can best be realized if the therapeutic stem cells and the tissues derived from them are genetically identical to the patient receiving them. Therefore, unless the patient is the source of the stem cells, the stem cells need to be "customized" by replacing the stem cell's genetic material with the patient's before cueing the stem cells to differentiate into a specific cell type. To date, this genetic material replacement and reprogramming can be done effectively only with embryonic stem cells.

Biotechnology vaccines

Vaccines help the body recognize and fight infectious diseases. Conventional vaccines use weakened or killed forms of a virus or bacteria to stimulate the immune system to create the antibodies that will provide resistance to the disease. Usually only one or a few proteins on the surface of the bacteria or virus, called antigens, trigger the production of antibodies. Biotechnology is helping us improve existing vaccines and create new vaccines against infectious agents, such as the viruses that cause cervical cancer and genital herpes.

Most of the new vaccines consist only of the antigen [immune stimulating substance], not the actual microbe [germ]. The vaccine is made by inserting the gene that produces the antigen into a manufacturing cell, such as yeast. During the manufacturing process, which is similar to brewing beer, each yeast cell makes a perfect copy of itself and the antigen gene. The antigen is later purified. By isolating antigens and producing them in the laboratory, it is possible to make vaccines that cannot transmit the virus or bacterium itself. This method also increases the amount of vaccine that can be manufactured because, unlike traditional vaccine production, biotechnology vaccines can be made without using live animals.

Using these techniques of biotechnology, scientists have developed antigen-only vaccines against life-threatening diseases such as hepatitis B and meningitis.

Recently we have discovered that injecting small pieces of DNA from microbes is sufficient for triggering antibody production. Such DNA vaccines could provide immunization against microbes for which we currently have no vaccines. DNA vaccines against HIV, malaria and the influenza virus are currently in clinical trials.

Biotechnology is also broadening the vaccine concept beyond protection against infectious organisms. Various researchers are developing vaccines against diseases such as diabetes, chronic inflammatory disease, Alzheimer's disease and cancers.

Whether the vaccine is a live virus, coat protein or a piece of DNA, vaccine production requires elaborate and costly facilities and procedures. And then there's the issue of painful injections. Industrial and academic researchers are using biotechnology to circumvent both of these problems with edible vaccines manufactured by plants and animals.

Genetically modified goats have produced a possible malaria vaccine in their milk. University researchers have obtained positive results using human volunteers who consumed hepatitis vaccines in bananas, and E. coli and cholera vaccines in potatoes. In addition, because these vaccines are genetically incorporated into food plants and need no refrigeration, sterilization equipment or needles, they may prove useful in developing countries.

Researchers are also developing skin patch vaccines for tetanus, anthrax and E. coli.

The future of medicine

While biotechnology has already had a significant impact on the diagnosis, treatment and prevention of diseases, the best is yet to come. We are entering a new era in medical research, disease diagnosis and health-care provision. . . .

These advances will bring about radically new approaches to health care The practice of medicine will be fundamentally changed, becoming more comprehensive and integrated, highly individualized and more preventive rather than simply therapeutic.

3

Genetic Engineering Will Be Used for Destructive Purposes

John Gray

John Gray is a professor of European thought at the London School of Economics. He is a former professor of politics at Oxford University and fellow of Jesus College, Oxford. He is a regular contributor to the Guardian *and the* Times Literary Supplement *and is the author of numerous academic articles and books, including* Straw Dogs: Thoughts on Humans and Other Animals.

Genetic engineering offers the promise of such things as cures for disease and the creation of a better world. However, although some people believe that humans will be able to use the powers given by new biotechnologies to create an enlightened society, it is more likely that they will be used for destructive purposes. Humanity will be unable to reach a global consensus on the uses of genetic engineering, and the development of science and technology will continue to be controlled by economic and military interests, as they have been throughout history. The insidious weapons created through biotechnology will be used in wars of unimaginable brutality. If genetic engineers manage to redesign human beings, the result will be creatures with the worst characteristics of humanity: vanity, greed, and savagery.

John Gray, "The Unstoppable March of Clones: We Have Failed to Control the Spread of Nuclear Weapons, So How Can We Hope to Control the Development of Designer Babies and Other Results of Biotechnology?" *New Statesman*, vol. 131, June 24, 2002. Copyright © 2002 by New Statesman, Ltd. Reproduced by permission.

[C ommunist leader] Fidel Castro has ordered Cuban biotechnologists to clone a new breed of cow. The ageing caudillo sees the cloning project, which attempts to replicate White Udder, a cow that became legendary for its milk output in the 1980s, as a solution to Cuba's chronic shortage of dairy products. The benefits to Castro of resurrecting the animal, which died 17 years ago, extend well beyond its impact on the milk industry. A successful cloning would be a coup for Cuban biotechnology, a pointed reminder to the US that it is not always in the vanguard of scientific development, and a boost to the prestige of a crumbling regime.

What lies ahead

The tangle of motives that has led Castro to become a cheerleader for biotechnology is a cautionary tale for anyone who imagines that the industry can be made subject to effective international regulation. In launching a scientific experiment for reasons that are at least partly political, Cuba's leader is doing what other countries have also done, and will surely do in the future. Such experiments are unlikely to be confined to nonhuman animals. Within the lifetimes of people who are alive today, it will become feasible to alter human nature. If we believe what we are told by scientists, biotechnology offers more than the promise of removing genetic defects that contribute to common diseases. It opens up the possibility of redesigning human beings. The present generation will be able to shape the next in ways that have never before been possible. As scientific knowledge grows, it seems likely that not only the disease profiles, but also the personalities of future human beings will become alterable by human will. At that point, equipped with the new powers conferred by biotechnology, we will be what [Russian Communist leader Vladimir] Lenin could only dream of becoming—engineers of souls.

Will biotechnology bring about a better world?

It is a prospect that evokes both excitement and foreboding. Belatedly acknowledging that history may not have ended, [author] Francis Fukuyama conjures up an intoxicating vision of a post-human future in which science enables us to reshape our very essence. But in his latest book, *Our Post-Human Future: Consequences of the Biotechnology Revolution*, he warns that, as a result of uneven access to the new technologies, a genetic underclass could come into being, greatly magnifying existing inequalities. Worse, as envisioned in Aldous Huxley's [novel] *Brave New World*, a new underclass could be bred deliberately, reintroducing something akin to slavery. These are real hazards; but, Fukuyama insists, they can be controlled by a well-constructed regime of regulation.

> *In [the] future, as in the past, the development of science and technology will be governed by war and profit.*

[Evolutionary biologist and author Edward Osborne] Wilson, on the other hand, while he acknowledges that the new technologies carry risks, argues that they open up a future of indefinite progress. In his books *Consilience: the Unity of Knowledge* and *The Future of Life*, Wilson declares that genetically modified crops can ease us through the environmental bottleneck created by the expanding numbers of human beings. Beyond that, genetic engineering makes possible what he calls "the conscious control of human evolution": a time when the jerry-built structures of human nature have been reconstructed, and humanity's development is no longer a matter of blind evolutionary drift.

Wilson and Fukuyama thus differ in their assessment of the comparative risks and benefits of the new technologies. Where they are at one is in their belief that humanity can master them. Here, they embody a paradox in contemporary thinking. For both men, humans are best understood in Darwinian terms of natural selection. Wilson, the greatest contemporary Darwinian and a genuinely profound thinker, is an ardent foe of the myth of exemptionalism—the belief that humans belong to a different order of things from the rest of the natural world. In their origins and nature, he argues, they are an animal species like any other. This is a conclusion that Fukuyama, who has made wide-ranging (if at times ill-judged) use of sociobiological theory, also accepts. Yet both thinkers are adamant that humans can control their future development; and that, using scientific knowledge, they can overcome the natural limits that frame the lives of other species. Humanity can use the powers given by new technology to bring about a world better than any that has ever existed.

This is faith, not science. By insisting that we can use our powers of invention to control and direct our future, these thinkers resurrect a religious image of humankind. According to Christians, other animals may be driven along in the natural drift of things, but humans can fashion their lives through autonomous choices. That—and not merely its prodigious inventiveness and awesome powers of destruction—is what marks humanity off from the rest of life. This Christian idea that humans are separated from other animals by an unbridgeable gulf is not found in all, or even most religions. It is absent from Hinduism and Buddhism, Taoism and Shinto. It is explicitly rejected in the primordial religion of mankind—animism—in which other animals figure on terms of equality with humans, if not superiority to them. Exemptionalism is a distinctively Judaeo-Christian doctrine. It is therefore not surprising that it should animate the political religions that have sprung up in the wake of Christianity's decline. . . .

> *How can we expect to regulate biotechnology when it has proved impossible to prevent the proliferation of weapons of mass destruction?*

Wilson's idea that humanity can take charge of its evolution makes sense only if you think it is different in kind from every other animal species. In each case, these beliefs are direct inheritances from religion.

History drives science

In *Our Posthuman Future*, Fukuyama announces "the recommencement of history" on the grounds that science makes possible the transformation of human nature, and thereby new historical conflicts. . . . But this is to turn the role of science in history upside down. It is not science that drives history, but history that drives science. Pure scientists may have developed nuclear physics, but nuclear fission came into the world as a by-product of war. The same is true of many advances in radar technology, medicine and other fields. The urgent necessities of military conflict brought them into being, and economic forces determined their subsequent development. The new biotechnologies will be no different. In [the] future, as in the past, the development of science and technology will be governed by war and profit. . . .

Can biotechnology be regulated?

A similar fallacy infects Fukuyama's prognostications on biotechnology. He believes that an international consensus on the proper uses of genetic engineering can manage its hazards. Yet he says little about how a consensus can be enforced. The world contains nearly 200 sovereign states, many collapsed or heavily corroded by crime or corruption, others ruled by capricious tyrants, still others locked in bitter conflicts. How can we expect to regulate biotechnology when it has proved impossible to prevent the proliferation of weapons of mass destruction?

The military uses of biotechnology could pose a threat comparable to nuclear war. Genetically selective weapons may be developed to target particular ethnic groups. Long-acting toxins may be devised that can devastate populations many years after being disseminated. Further ahead, reproductive cloning may be used to mass-manufacture soldiers more immune to emotions of sympathy and self-preservation than even today's suicide bombers. The development and spread of new weapons of mass destruction is a side effect of the growth of knowledge interacting with primordial human needs. That is why, finally, it is unstoppable. The same is true of genetic engineering. If people try, during the coming century, to redesign human beings, they will not do so on the basis of an enlightened international consensus. It will occur haphazardly, as part of competition and conflict among states, business corporations and criminal networks. The new, post-human creatures that may emerge from these murky rivalries will not be ideal types embodying the best human ideals: they will reproduce some of the worst features of unregenerate humanity.

A utopian view of humanity

When E.O. Wilson writes of humanity taking charge of its evolution, he enunciates the core belief of scientific humanism. Like other humanists, however, he has forgotten an important implication of Darwin's teachings: "humanity" does not exist.

The upshot of the theory of natural selection is that the human species is an accidental assemblage of genes, continuously mutating under the impact of changes in the environment. It is no more a collective entity capable of making decisions about its future than any other animal species. Wilson's failure to grasp this truth gives his proposals for dealing with the environmental crisis an unmistakably utopian quality. He presents irrefutable evidence that human activity is wreaking great damage on the planet, and exterminating other living things at a rate unknown since the end of the dinosaurs. By his estimate, half the earth's plant and animal species will be gone by the end of the century. Yet, despite this overwhelming evidence of human fecklessness, Wilson insists that salvation can be found in science. Using new technologies, including genetically modified foods, the swelling human population can be fed. With population control and environmental conservation, the destruction of biodiversity can be arrested.

> *Humans . . . use their growing knowledge in the service of their most urgent needs—however conflicting, or ultimately destructive, these may prove to be.*

Wilson's programme is admirable; but it expresses a strangely unscientific, indeed irrational, faith in the human capacity for cooperation. If we look to history, we find no reason to think that science will ever be used to achieve a sustainable balance with the environment. The limits of growth are re-emerging as a major source of geostrategic conflict. As Wilson notes, since 1960, human numbers have doubled to around six billion. Barring catastrophes, they will rise by another two to four billion later this century. In the Gulf—a region entirely dependent on depleting supplies of oil fonts income—the population will double in about 20 years. It does not take much insight into human behaviour to see that this is hardly a scenario for global co-operation. The combination of rising human numbers, dwindling natural resources and spreading weapons of mass destruction is more likely to unleash wars of unprecedented savagery. If we can bring ourselves to look clearly at this prospect, we will lay aside utopian fantasies of global co-operation. We will see our task as staving off disaster from day to day.

To account for the Fukuyama/Wilson faith that mankind can achieve conscious mastery of its evolution, we need to look back at 19th-century cult-French positivism. Led by thinkers such as Henri Saint-Simon and Auguste Comte, the positivists were the inventors of the religion of humanity that has inspired the secular religions of the past two centuries. They had many eccentricities, including a version of the Catholic practice of crossing oneself in which they tapped the parts of the cranium believed by phrenologists to be connected with order and progress, but their religion has been vastly influential. It inspired not only [Communist revolutionary Karl] Marx but also, through [English philosopher] John Stuart Mill, many liberals, and it stands behind the faith in progress that is shared by all parties today.

Biotechnology will fall prey to human motives

Humanists believe their faith in progress is founded on reason, but it is not a result of scientific inquiry. It is the Judaeo-Christian idea of history as a universal narrative of salvation dressed up in secular clothes. Progressives believe that the growth of knowledge leads to the emancipation of humanity. If we peel away the moth-eaten brocade of progressive hope, we find that humans are highly inventive animals, who use their growing knowledge in the service of their most urgent needs—however conflicting, or ultimately destructive, these may prove to be. They will use the new biotechnologies as they have used previous scientific developments. If the advance of reproductive cloning produces a new breed of post-humans, it will come about from the interplay of all-too-human forces and motives—war, profit and the vanity of leaders. The post-human future will not be the moment when humanity takes charge of its future. It will be just another blind turn in human history.

4

Human Germ Line Engineering Is Unethical

Richard Hayes

Richard Hayes is executive director of the Center for Genetics and Society, a nonprofit public affairs organization supporting responsible social control of the new human genetic technologies. He previously served as national director of volunteer development and assistant political director for the Sierra Club. Hayes has also worked as a political organizer for a wide range of environmental and social organizations.

Human germ line engineering (HGE), making genetic changes in people that will be passed on to future generations, is rapidly gaining acceptance. Supporters envision a future where people can choose preferred traits for their children. Over time, the genetically enhanced would become a privileged separate species. Allowing this technology to be developed would not only bring profound social and political changes, but would also forever change the nature of what it means to be human. Yet the opposition to human germ line engineering has been almost nonexistent because it is so new and there is little public understanding of its horrifying implications. Furthermore, people falsely associate it only with the eradication of disease and alleviation of human suffering. Humanity needs to recognize the enormous threat posed by HGE technology and organize to impose a global ban on its development.

Richard Hayes, "The Quiet Campaign for Genetically Engineered Humans," *Earth Island Journal*, vol. 16, Spring 2001, p. 28. Copyright © 2001 by the Earth Island Institute. Reproduced by permission.

W e are fast approaching the most consequential technological threshold in all of human history: the ability to
directly manipulate the genes we pass on to our children.

Development and use of these technologies would irrevo-
cably change the nature of human life and human society. It
would destabilize human biological identity and function. It
would put into play a wholly unprecedented set of social, psychological and political forces that would feed back upon
themselves with impacts quite beyond our ability to imagine,
much less control.

These technologies are being developed and promoted by
an influential network of scientists who see themselves usher-
ing in a new epoch for human life on Earth. They look forward
to the day when parents can quite literally assemble their children from genes listed in a catalog. They celebrate a future in
which our common humanity is lost as a genetically enhanced
elite increasingly acquires the attributes of a separate species.

There is little public awareness of the full implications of
the new human genetic engineering (HGE) technologies or of
the campaign to promote them. There are few popular institutions and no social or political movements that are addressing
the immense challenges these technologies pose.

Somatic vs. germline engineering

While some applications of HGE are benign and hold great potential for preventing disease and alleviating human suffering,
other applications could open the door to a human future
more horrific than our worst nightmares.

Two very different applications of genetic engineering must
be distinguished. One application changes the genes in cells in
your body other than your egg and sperm cells. Such changes are
not passed to any children you may have. Applications of this
sort are currently in clinical trials and are generally considered
socially acceptable. The technical term for this application is "somatic" genetic engineering (after the Greek "soma" for "body").

The other application of genetic engineering changes the
genes in eggs, sperm, or very early embryos. This affects not
only any children you might have, but also all succeeding generations. It opens the door to the reconfiguration of the human
species. The technical term for this application is "germline"
genetic engineering (because eggs and sperm are the "germi-
nal" or "germline" cells).

Many advocates of germline engineering say it is needed to allow couples to avoid passing on genetic diseases such as cystic fibrosis or sickle cell anemia. This is simply not true. Far less consequential methods (such as pre-natal and pre-implantation screening) already exist to accomplish this same goal. Germline manipulation is necessary only if you wish to "enhance" your children with genes they wouldn't be able to get from you or your partner.

Germline engineering gains momentum

The ability to directly manipulate plant and animal genes was developed during the late 1970's. Proposals to begin human gene manipulation were put forth in the early 1980's and aroused much controversy. A small number of researchers argued in favor of germline manipulation, but the majority of scientists and others opposed it. In 1983, a letter signed by 53 religious leaders declared that genetic engineering of the human germline "represents a fundamental threat to the preservation of the human species as we know it, and should be opposed with the same courage and conviction as we now oppose the threat of nuclear extinction."

In 1985, the US National Institutes of Health (NIH) approved somatic gene therapy trials, but said that it would not accept proposals for germline manipulation "at present." That ambiguous decision did little to discourage advocates of germline engineering, who knew that somatic experiments were the critical first step toward HGE experiments. Following the first approved clinical attempts at somatic gene therapy in 1990, advocates of germline engineering began writing advocacy pieces in medical, ethical, legal and other journals to build broader support.

By the mid- and late-1990's, the progress of the federally funded Human Genome Project in locating all 80,000-plus human genes fueled speculation about eventual applications, including germline engineering.

In 1996, scientists cloned the first genetic duplicate of an adult mammal (the sheep "Dolly"). In 1999, researchers mastered the techniques for disassembling human embryos and keeping embryonic cells alive in laboratory cultures. These developments made it possible, for the first time, to imagine a procedure whereby the human germline could be engineered in a commercially practicable manner.

HGE advocates were further encouraged by the social, cultural and political conditions of the late 1990's—a period characterized by technological enthusiasm, distrust of government regulation, the spread of consumerist/competitive/libertarian values, and the perceived weakened ability of national governments to enforce laws and treaties, as a result of globalization.

> *// Some applications of HGE . . . could open the door to a human future more horrific than our worst nightmares. //*

In March 1998, Gregory Stock, director of the Program on Medicine, Technology and Society at the University of California at Los Angeles (UCLA), organized a symposium on "Engineering the Human Germline." It was attended by nearly 1,000 people and received front-page coverage in *The New York Times* and *The Washington Post*. All the speakers were avid proponents of germline engineering.

Four months later, one of the symposium's key participants, HGE pioneer W. French Anderson, submitted a draft proposal to the NIH to begin somatic gene transfer experiments on human fetuses. He acknowledged that this procedure would have a "relatively high" potential for "inadvertent gene transfer to the germline." Anderson's proposal was widely acknowledged to be strategically crafted so that approval could be construed as acceptance of germline modification, at least in some circumstances. . . .

A newly emerging ideology

Advocacy of germline engineering and techno-eugenics (i.e., technologically enabled human genetic manipulation and selection) is an integral element of a newly emerging sociopolitical ideology. This ideology is gaining acceptance among scientific, high-tech, media and policy elites. A key foundational text is the book *Remaking Eden: How Cloning and Beyond Will Change the Human Family*, by Princeton University molecular biologist Lee Silver. Silver looks forward to a future in which the health, appearance, personality, cognitive ability, sensory capacity and the lifespan of our children all become artifacts of genetic manipulation. Silver acknowledges that financial constraints will limit their widespread adoption, so that over time society will segregate into the "GenRich" and the "Naturals."

In Silver's vision of the future:

> The GenRich—who account for ten percent of the American population—all carry synthetic genes. All aspects of the economy, the media, the entertainment industry, and the knowledge industry are controlled by members of the GenRich class. . . .

> Naturals work as low-paid service providers or as laborers. . . . [Eventually] the GenRich class and the Natural class will become entirely separate species with no ability to crossbreed, and with as much romantic interest in each other as a current human would have for a chimpanzee. . . .

> Many think that it is inherently unfair for some people to have access to technologies that can provide advantages while others, less well-off, are forced to depend on chance alone . . . [but] American society adheres to the principle that personal liberty and personal fortune are the primary determinants of what individuals are allowed and able to do.

> Indeed, in a society that values individual freedom above all else, it is hard to find any legitimate basis for restricting the use of repro-genetics [reproductive genetic technologies]. . . . I will argue [that] the use of reprogenetic technologies is inevitable. . . . Whether we like it or not, the global marketplace will reign supreme.

Impact on the environment

HGE enthusiasts typically anticipate a future in which genetic technology permeates, transforms and reconfigures all sectors of the natural world—plants, animals, humans and ecosystems. Many look forward to what they call the "Singularity"— that point in the next few decades when any distinction between the natural and the technological has been completely dissolved. Many couple their enthusiasm for genetic engineering with an explicit disparagement of environmentalist values.

Nobel Laureate James Watson, for example, has complained that "ever since we achieved a breakthrough in the area of re-combinant DNA in 1973, left-wing nuts and environmental kooks have been screaming that we will create some kind of Frankenstein bug or Andromeda strain that will destroy us all."

[Scientist and author] Gregory Stock has stated: "Even if half the world's species were lost, enormous diversity would still remain. . . . When those in the distant future look back on this period of history, they will likely see it not as the era when the natural environment was impoverished, but as the age when a plethora of new forms—some biological, some techno-logical, some a combination of the two—burst onto the scene. . . . We best serve ourselves, as well as future generations, by fo-cusing on the short-term consequences of our actions rather than our vague notions about the needs of the distant future."

It is difficult to see how a society that accepts the techno-eugenic re-engineering of the human species will maintain any sense of humility, reverence and respect regarding the rest of the natural world.

Promoting HGE technologies

Supporters of human germline engineering and cloning have established institutes to spread their vision. In addition to Stock's program at UCLA, the Los Angeles–based Extropy Insti-tute holds workshops on how to organize politically to advance the "post-human" agenda, including sessions on how to talk to the press and public about human genetic modification in ways that build support and diffuse opposition. In 1999, the Maryland-based Human Biodiversity Institute presented a sem-inar on the prospects for genetically modified humans at a Hudson Institute retreat attended by former British Prime Min-ister Margaret Thatcher.

Meanwhile, the biotech industry is actively developing the technologies that would make it possible to offer human germline engineering on a commercial basis. This work is al-most completely unregulated. Geron Corporation of Menlo Park, California, holds patents on human embryo manipula-tion and cloning techniques. Advanced Cell Technologies of Worcester, Massachusetts, announced in 1999 that it had cre-ated a human/bovine embryo by implanting the nucleus of a human cell into the egg of a cow. No laws exist that would have prevented this trans-species embryo from being implanted in a woman's uterus in an attempt to bring a baby to term. Such a child would have contained a small but significant proportion of cow genes.

Chromos Molecular Systems, Inc., in British Columbia, is developing artificial human chromosomes that would enable the engineering of multiple complex traits. People whose germlines were engineered with artificial chromosomes, and who wanted to pass complete sets of these to their children intact, would only be able to mate with others carrying the same artificial chromosomes. This condition, called "reproductive isolation," is the primary criterion that biologists use to classify a population as a separate species.

Little organized opposition exists

Given the enormity of what is at stake and the fact that advocates of the new techno-eugenics are hardly coy about their intentions, it is remarkable that organized opposition has been all but absent. Why is this?

One reason is that the most critical technologies have been developed only within the last three years or so—there simply hasn't been time for people to fully understand their implications and respond.

Further, the prospect of re-designing the human species is beyond anything that humanity has ever before had to confront. People have trouble taking this seriously—it seems fantastical and beyond the limits of what anyone would actually do or that society would allow.

> *Advanced Cell Technologies . . . created a human/bovine embryo by implanting the nucleus of a human cell into the egg of a cow.*

In addition, attitudes concerning human genetic engineering don't fit neatly along the familiar ideological axes of right/left or conservative/liberal. The additional axis of libertarian/communitarian attitudes is needed to fully categorize currently contending socio-politico commitments. The libertarian right and libertarian left tend to consider human genetic modification as a property right or as an individual right, respectively. By contrast, the communitarian right and communitarian left tend to be strongly opposed—the former typically for reasons grounded in religious beliefs and the latter out of concern for human dignity, social equity and solidarity.

> *Advocates of the techno-eugenic future are racing to create designer babies . . . before people realize what is happening and what is at stake.*

Finally, although people sense that the new genetic technologies are likely to introduce profound social and political challenges, they also associate these technologies with the promise of miracle cures. Before any sentiment in favor of banning certain uses of genetic technology can take root, people will have to understand that this would not foreclose means of preventing or curing genetic diseases.

Banning human germline engineering

The core policies that humanity will need to adopt are straightforward: we will need global bans on altering the genes we pass to our children and on creating human clones. We'll also need effective, accountable systems for regulating those HGE technologies (such as somatic genetic manipulation) that have desirable applications but could be dangerously abused.

Many countries, including France, Germany and India, already have banned both germline engineering and cloning. The Council of Europe is working to have these banned in all 41 of its member countries. The United Nations and UNESCO have called for a global ban on human cloning and a World Health Organization study has called for a global ban on germline engineering.

The base of any effective global movement to bring the new human genetic technologies under societal control will, as always, be strong activist civil society organizations. Among the most important of these are the environmental and Green organizations. In 1999, Friends of the Earth President Brent Blackwelder and Physicians for Social Responsibility Executive Director Robert Musil circulated a statement that declared:

> We believe that certain activities in the area of ge-
> netics and cloning should be prohibited because
> they violate basic environmental and ethical prin-
> ciples. . . . We believe that germline manipulations,
> for their ability to change whole generations, not
> just individuals, go far beyond the boundaries of
> human scientific and ethical understanding and
> are too dangerous for human civilization to pursue.
> . . . Being a product of scientific design and manip-
> ulation as opposed to natural chance will funda-
> mentally change the place of the individual in so-
> ciety and would profoundly alter the relationship
> of human beings to the natural world.

In February 2000, nearly 250 concerned leaders, including
environmentalists Bill McKibben, Amory Lovins, Terry Tem-
pest Williams, Gary Snyder and Mark Dowie, signed an open
letter warning that the prospect of human germline engi-
neenng "represents a point of decision—one that ranks among
the most consequential that humanity will ever make. We
should acknowledge that human germline engineering is an
unneeded technology that poses horrific risks, and adopt policies to ban it."

The next few years will be critical. Advocates of the techno-
eugenic future are racing to create designer babies and human
clones before people realize what is happening and what is at
stake. They believe that once humanity is presented with such
fait accompli, resistance will crumble and the new epoch will
have been launched. It is imperative that those who value the
beauty, vitality and wonder of the natural world begin orga-
nizing now to ensure that human beings do not become technological artifacts.

5

Agricultural Biotechnology Provides Many Benefits Worldwide

Maureen A. Mackey and Charles R. Santerre

Maureen A. Mackey is in charge of nutrition regulatory affairs for the agricultural biotechnology company Monsanto. Before joining Monsanto, she was a nutritionist at food industry giant Kellogg Company. She earned her doctoral degree in nutritional science from the University of Minnesota. Charles R. Santerre is an associate professor in the Department of Foods and Nutrition at Purdue University, and an adjunct associate professor in the environmental science program at Ohio State University. He has published numerous academic articles about nutritional science.

Conventional agriculture will not be adequate to meet ever-increasing global food demands. However, the use of genetically modified (GM) crops will increase food supplies, provide more nutritious food, and protect the environment. Unfortunately, a lack of information about the many advantages of agricultural biotechnology and the safety of GM foods creates fear and misperceptions. However, such fear is unjustified because of the regulatory processes that assure food safety. Scientists use precise and controlled methods to transfer genes to create crops with desirable characteristics. Genetically engineered crops are already improving much of the global food supply in a number of ways. These crops are resistant to pests and viruses and require fewer herbicides than traditional crops. As with any new technology, scientists need to continue to evaluate the potential health risks of biotechnology. So far several crops have received positive evaluations, and others are expected to be approved in the next few years.

It is increasingly clear that the use of biotechnology in agriculture will have profound implications for agriculture, the environment, and the global economy. It is already impacting the world's food supply. The first wave of genetically improved products has largely included major food commodity crops, such as soybeans and corn, as well as cotton. These genetic changes help plants protect themselves against pests or make them tolerant to herbicides used to control weeds. The economic benefits for farmers have been seen, and data are confirming that genetically improved crops benefit the environment by reducing reliance on insecticides and herbicides. Scientists are working on the next wave of products that will include direct consumer benefits, such as increased levels of vitamins in fruits and vegetables, improved amino acid or fatty acid profiles, or improved texture and taste.

However, a lack of information about biotechnology and its potential to help farmers produce more food and more nutritious food while protecting the environment has led to misperceptions and fear about biotechnology-produced products. Hence, it is important to understand what biotechnology is and how it can be used to develop solutions for tomorrow's world. . . .

Biotechnology is more efficient than traditional methods

Many of the techniques used in biotechnology today are not new but are more precise and more rapid versions of traditional methods used throughout history. From the time agriculture began, farmers created better plants by selectively breeding plants that were the highest yield producers with those least susceptible to disease. Farmers also selectively bred meat and dairy animals as well as birds—seeking to increase meat, milk, and egg yield while reducing feed cost; without knowing it, these farmers were practicing a form of biotechnology. Although hybridization achieved through conventional breeding programs has been, and will continue to be, extremely valuable, there are limitations to this process. In plant breeding, the conventional practice combines all genes of the parent plants and results in progeny that have both desirable and undesirable traits. To eliminate undesirable traits, plant breeders must "back cross" the new plant varieties with other plants over several generations. This is both time consuming and expensive. One advantage of plant biotechnology is that it is possible to transfer only the desired gene(s) encoding the desired trait(s) into new plants in a more precise and controlled manner within a relatively short period. Plant biotechnology also enables the transfer of genes from nonplant organisms, such as bacteria, to plants, as well as between plants that are not sexually compatible. For example, genes from naturally occurring soil bacteria have been inserted into several crop plants to enable them to protect themselves against insect pests.

Methods of genetically modifying plants

A primer on the techniques involved in biotechnology shows how foods with new characteristics can be produced. Scientists can identify specific genes responsible for certain traits or physiologic functions in an organism. A specific gene segment containing a desired trait is obtained from a donor organism, other DNA [deoxyribonucleic acid] sequences are added to enable expression in the recipient organism, and the entire DNA sequence is transferred into a recipient cell, where it can be expressed and duplicated. The "cutting and pasting" of DNA is achieved through the use of enzyme "scissors" isolated from bacteria. These enzymes, or restriction endonucleases, occur naturally in organisms and perform vital functions. Hundreds of restriction enzymes have been isolated and are commercially available for cleaving DNA at specific DNA sequences, permitting the precise removal of a DNA sequence.

There are several ways to accomplish gene insertion in plants, with the most popular being through use of bacterial plasmids or a particle gun. Plasmids are rings of DNA found in bacteria. A gene coding for a desired trait from a donor cell is spliced into the bacteria's plasmid by use of the enzyme "scissors" described. Specific bacterial plasmids are particularly useful because they can transfer genetic material into plant cells. For example, researchers have isolated a gene that codes for a protein that provides viral disease resistance to plants. This gene, along with regulatory sequences that enable gene function in plants, has been transferred into the plasmid of the soil bacterium Agrobacterium tumefaciens. When the bacteria are added to cells of plants such as potato or tomato, the gene for viral resistance is transferred into and stably maintained in the plant cells. The result is potato or tomato plants that are now resistant to a specific viral disease. Similar disease resistance can be developed by use of traditional breeding methods, but this development is both tedious and costly.

For corn, wheat, and soybean plants, researchers have also used a "particle gun" to transfer desirable traits. Pellets of gold or tungsten are coated with the desired DNA and literally fired through the plant cell walls. As they pass through the cells, some of the DNA coating is left behind and stably incorporated into the plant DNA to create a genetically improved plant cell that will now express the desired trait. These plant cells are then grown in culture to form plants that are grown first in greenhouses and then in field trials. The ideal genetically modified plant will have all the desirable traits of the parent plant, such as high yield, as well as consistent and effective expression of the inserted trait.

Genetically improved crops

The first genetically improved crop was the Flavr Savr[TM] tomato, approved for commercial sale in the United States in 1994. The rationale for such a product was simple: conventional tomatoes are picked green and hard so they can withstand the rigors of harvesting and transportation. En route to supermarkets, they are exposed to ethylene gas to artificially ripen them, but this treatment does nothing to promote flavor development. Calgene, a biotechnology company in California, engineered tomatoes such that the enzyme that degrades pectin and produces softness is inhibited. This allows tomatoes to develop vine-ripened aroma and flavor yet remain firm longer than conventional tomatoes. The consumer benefits from this because a flavorful product with ideal tomato characteristics is produced.

From 1986 to 1997, approximately 25,000 field trials involving 60 transgenic [carrying DNA sequences not normally in its genome] plant species were conducted in 45 countries. Genetically improved corn is by far the most frequent crop that has been tested in field trials, followed by tomato, soybean, potato, and cotton. In addition, other tested genetically improved plants include rice, cantaloupe, squash, and yams. The most frequently tested traits are herbicide tolerance, insect resistance, viral, fungal and bacterial resistance, food quality enhancement, and nutritional improvement. Plant products with multiple traits (eg, insect and virus protection, insect protection, and herbicide tolerance) have been generated by combining traits through traditional breeding methods.

Economic impact

Global commercial production of genetically modified plants in 1999 reached an estimated 98.6 million acres. Twelve countries (United States, Argentina, Canada, China, Australia, South Africa, Mexico, Spain, France, Portugal, Romania, and Ukraine) grew seven crops (soybean, corn, cotton, canola, potato, squash, papaya). Global sales of transgenic crops have risen from $75 million in 1995 to more than $2 billion in 1999. Over 55% of the soybeans, 45% of the cotton, and 35% of the corn grown in the United States in 1999 were genetically modified. If the traditionally improved crops are included, the percentage production approaches 100%. Few farmers grow crops using unimproved seed.

These products have significant economic value. In 1997, glyphosate-tolerant soybeans created a global economic value of over $1 billion, and insect-protected cotton grown in the United States created an economic value of approximately $240 million in 1996 and $190 million in 1997. Farmers received the greatest portion of this value, with an estimated 76% of the value for glyphosate-tolerant soybeans in 1997, 59% of the value of insect-protected cotton in 1996, and 42% in 1997.

A growing global food demand

Global demand for food is projected to at least double and possibly triple as a result of projected increases in the world's population from 6 billion in 1999 to approximately 10 billion people by the mid-21st century. The situation is even more dire in developing areas of the world, such as in Africa, where a 300% increase in food supplies will be required, and in Asia and Latin America where 69% and 80% increases, respectively, will be needed. In addition, as the middle class grows in developing countries, there likely will be increased demand for meat, milk, and other animal-based products. Thus, there will be increased need for animal feeds.

We are already in a situation in which over one billion people, especially in the developing world, do not have enough food to eat on a daily basis, with half of those people suffering serious malnutrition. In addition to the problem of insufficient energy intake, there are widespread deficiencies in certain vitamins and minerals, especially vitamin A and iron. According to the World Bank, "The main challenge is to expand agricultural production at a rate exceeding population growth in the decades ahead so as to provide food to the hungry new mouths to feed." The World Bank outlined a potential list of agricultural improvements that can help solve this problem, including improving pest control, soil conservation, developing new crop strains with increased yields, resistance to pests, tolerance to drought conditions, and reducing dependency on pesticides and herbicides. Modern plant biotechnology will be an important tool for achieving this goal of increasing the food supply.

Increased crop productivity

Several factors besides population growth have decreased arable land globally over the past 30 years, and arable land is expected to continue to fall. As the population grows and places pressure on land used for farming, the abundance of arable land will decrease. However, most of the growth in the world's population is in developing countries, which have the least potential to expand arable land. Thus, increasing the productivity of crops is the only significant means for increasing food production. In addition, it will be imperative that a globally sustainable agriculture system be developed that will conserve natural resources and increase productivity in an environmentally friendly manner.

Conventional technology alone will not be adequate to provide sufficient feed and food for the burgeoning global population. For example, despite the fact that approximately $32 billion is spent annually on conventional pesticides, pests still reduce global food production by at least one third, which is the equivalent of 1.5 billion tons of food. Biotechnology solutions are available to decrease the impact of these pests; pest-protected crops have now been commercialized in a number of countries. For example, farmers in the United States who planted Bacillus thuringiensis (Bt)-treated corn realized a yield increase of 60 million bushels, or 4.3 bushels per acre. The increased crop yields (up to about 25%) from genetically modified plants will have a significant impact on the world's food production.

> *Many of the techniques used in biotechnology today are not new but are more precise and more rapid versions of traditional methods used throughout history.*

In the future, crops could be genetically improved to withstand heat, drought, and soils with high salt and mineral content. Productivity also could be increased by improving the quality of seed grains, increasing plant fertility, and developing shorter plant breeding cycles. Increased food supplies could be achieved by developing foods that could be dried and rehydrated without loss of flavor and by protecting against postharvest losses caused by storage insects and disease. Crops improved through biotechnology have the potential to help insure the world against widespread famine.

Fewer insecticides, greater yields

Farmers are constantly faced with the formidable task of preventing or controlling crop insect infestation. For example, the Colorado potato beetle can quickly destroy a field of potato plants unless farmers frequently apply insecticide. Despite insecticide applications, much of the crop still may be lost to insect pests.

Insect-protected potato, cotton, and corn plants have been developed through the introduction of genes from the naturally occurring soil bacterium Bacillus thuringiensis (Bt). For several decades, Bt has been effectively and safely used as a biologic insecticidal spray on plant foliage, and as the insecticide of choice for organic farmers. A class of proteins produced by the bacteria is toxic to certain insects but harmless to humans, animals, and beneficial insects such as honeybees. However, several limitations of Bt insecticides include cost, degradability in sunlight, inactivation by rain, the need to be on the plant when the insect pest is feeding, and the need for repeated applications. Introducing Bt genes directly into the plants' genome overcomes these disadvantages.

Several companies have developed Bt crops, including cotton, potato, and corn. Use of these improved plants has maintained or increased crop yields and significantly reduced the use of chemical insecticides. For example, in the United States in 1997, farmers who planted genetically improved cotton used 300,000 fewer gallons of chemical insecticides to control cotton bollworm, tobacco budworm, and pink bollworm, the major insect pests of cotton. [It has been] estimated that over 2 million pounds of chemical insecticides have not been needed in the 3 years since the introduction of Bt cotton in the United States in 1996. Despite the decreased use of insecticides, these growers realized a significant increase in yield and an economic benefit of about $40 per acre with the genetically improved cotton compared with growers who planted conventional cotton. Growers in other countries have realized even greater economic value (up to $140/acre in China) and have reduced chemical insecticide use even more so than in the United States. For example, in Australia and China, chemical insecticide use was reduced by 48% and 60% to 80%, respectively, in fields planted with Bt cotton when compared with conventional cotton. In addition to these savings, there have been dramatic savings in production costs of these chemical insecticides and the packaging required to transport these products, reduced exposures to applicators, and reduced fuel to apply chemical insecticides. Another advantage of decreased reliance on chemical pesticides is the resulting decrease in migration of these compounds into surface and ground water.

> *Conventional technology alone will not be adequate to provide sufficient feed and food for the burgeoning global population.*

Research has expanded both the number of crops and the range of insects that can be controlled by genetically improved plants. These plants provide farmers an effective and environmentally preferred alternative to the frequent use of chemical insecticides. Insect-resistant plants are bred specifically to control the targeted insects. This method also allows farmers to maintain or increase the populations of beneficial insects that would have been eliminated with broad-spectrum pesticides.

Virus-resistant plant varieties

Viral, fungal, and bacterial diseases also can devastate crop yields and spoil crops during storage. To minimize these losses, farmers use chemical insecticides to control insects, such as aphids, which carry viruses, and fungicides to control the spread of fungi. In the United States, as much as 80% of crook neck squash can be destroyed by viruses. Plant biotechnologists have developed virus-resistant varieties of crook neck squash that provide resistance to two or three different plant viruses. Genetically improved squash plants allow farmers to plant one acre of squash, instead of the usual five acres to recover a single acre's yield. This greatly reduces the amounts of fertilizer, water, fuel, and chemical sprays needed for adequate crop yields. Consumers also will benefit from a consistent supply of squash during the summer and early fall months when the aphids that are viral vectors [used to transmit genetic material] are most active. As well, planting only one acre of squash allows the farmer to plant other desired food crops, thus increasing the variety of foods in the marketplace.

> *Biotechnology offers the opportunity to increase the nutritional value of foods or even add nutrients associated with specific health benefits.*

Viral protection strategies are being evaluated in watermelons, cantaloupes, cucumbers, potatoes, tomatoes, alfalfa, and other crops. Scientists in countries such as China, Chile, Argentina, Cuba, Kenya, and Malaysia are developing disease-resistant crops that are specific to their regions and diets. A particular case-in-point is the sweet potato, which is a staple food for many developing countries around the world, including Kenya and Uganda. In Africa, the feathery mottle virus (FMV) ruins two-thirds of the typical sweet potato harvest. Aphids also carry this virus, but many African farmers cannot afford the chemical insecticides needed to control the spread of aphid infestation. Availability of FMV-resistant sweet potato plants would be an economic boon to areas of Africa that are often plagued with food shortages and malnutrition.

Genetically modified crops are environmentally friendly

Weed control continues to be a major agricultural problem affecting crop yield. In developed countries, chemical herbicides are relied on to control weeds for most of the acreage of major crops. The ideal herbicide would be able to kill a broad array of weeds without harming crops or the environment. Genetically improved crops have been developed to be tolerant to glyphosate, an environmentally preferred herbicide. These crops, such as glyphosate-tolerant soybeans, can be planted in fields and treated with glyphosate to kill weeds on an "as-needed" basis. Glyphosate treatment means that farmers can use fewer herbicides and will likely need less total herbicide throughout the growing season. Again, this translates into less migration of herbicides into ground or surface waters, less soil erosion and compaction, better soil aeration, and reduced fuel combustion.

Farmers also depend on nitrogen fertilizers to boost crop yield. However, of the millions of pounds of fertilizer applied each year, only about half are actually used by plants. The remaining nitrogen ends up in soil and water and can result in environmental problems. Plant breeders are working on ways to increase a plant's efficiency in the uptake and use of nitrogen from the air and soil. This may allow farmers to decrease the use of chemical fertilizers, which in turn would result in less nitrogen entering soil and ground water. This reduction in fertilizer need would reduce the energy need for fertilizer production. In third-world agrarian nations, this is an important consideration.

Genetically modified foods are beneficial to diet and health

In recent years, the link between diet and health has become increasingly apparent. Numerous studies have associated the intake of specific nutrients such as unsaturated fat, fiber, vitamin C, vitamin E, carotenoids, and phytochemicals with reducing the risk of chronic diseases. Biotechnology offers the opportunity to increase the nutritional value of foods or even add nutrients associated with specific health benefits. Scientists are now modifying soybean, corn, and canola plants so the oils derived from these plants have improved fatty acid profiles. Squash, tomatoes, and potatoes could be grown to contain higher levels of vitamins C and E, and beta carotene, and plants could be improved to contain more compounds with cholesterol-lowering properties.

In developing countries, where malnutrition is a major concern, enhancing the nutritional content of staple foods may improve nutritional status and reduce the risk of disease. For example, the World Health Organization estimates that vitamin A deficiency affects over 250 million children worldwide, causing night blindness and vulnerability to disease. Plants genetically improved to contain increased amounts of beta carotene, the precursor of vitamin A, may play an important role in solving this problem. Consumption of 300 g genetically modified rice, which contains increased levels of beta carotene, could satisfy the RDA [recommended daily allowance] for vitamin A.

> *To illustrate the extent of regulatory and scientific review of plant biotechnology products, 27 different regulatory agencies reviewed the safety of soybeans.*

Iron-deficiency anemia is another widespread nutritional problem that could be mitigated by plant biotechnology. Researchers have modified rice to contain higher levels of bioavailable iron.

Since agriculture began, farmers have sought to improve the quality of their products through plant hybridization. Biotechnology makes it possible to achieve these effects much sooner and with more precision. An example of a product enhancement feature that is being developed by scientists is controlling the ripening process of tropical fruits, tomatoes, and peppers so these foods can be shipped without losing their fresh quality and taste. The ability to slow down the softening process will increase the year-round availability of fruits and vegetables that were once considered seasonal.

Existing products, such as insect-protected Bt corn, can also provide significant improvements in the quality of corn grain. Depending on the environmental conditions, corn grain can contain high levels of mycotoxins, including fumonisin. Research at Iowa State University has clearly shown that corn containing the Bt gene has significantly reduced levels of the fungal infection and significantly reduced levels of fumonisin, reductions of over 90% under some environmental conditions. Mycotoxins, including fumonisins, pose considerable health risks to the consumer. The resulting grain is safer to use and of higher quality for animal feed use.

Safety assessment and regulation

Are foods from genetically modified plants as safe as foods from traditional plant varieties? Could features of a plant be changed inadvertently during genetic engineering? For example, could the plant's nutrients, inherent toxicants (e.g., soybean trypsin inhibitor), or allergens be unfavorably changed? How should these products be tested to assess their safety? These questions have been considered by scientists and regulatory agencies both in the United States and internationally for over a decade, and safety assessment strategies have been recommended for the developers of such products by the International Food Biotechnology Council, the Food and Agriculture Organization, the World Health Organization, the Organization for Economic Cooperation and Development, the International Life Sciences Institute, and the US Food and Drug Administration (FDA).

In the United States, the FDA concluded in 1992 that the safety assessment process should focus on the final product and not on the genetic modification process. A food derived from a genetically modified crop that can be shown to be the same as that from the parent plant, with the exception of the introduced trait, is referred to as "substantially equivalent." For example, herbicide-tolerant soybeans were shown to be substantially equivalent to their parent soybeans except for the inserted protein that confers the tolerance to glyphosate. This equivalence was scientifically established by performing over 1,800 different analyses of the plant's compositional or nutritional characteristics, such as the levels of macronutrients, amino acids, fatty acids, anti-nutrients, and key vitamins and minerals; the results showed that there were no significant compositional changes in the soybeans caused by introducing the new gene or expressing the new protein. Further safety assessment then focused on the safety of the newly expressed protein, which constitutes approximately 0.1% of the total protein of the plant. The introduced protein is a member of a family of proteins that occur in every plant, bacteria, and fungi, and therefore has a long history of safe consumption. The safety of this specific protein was confirmed by evaluating its function and specificity, by performing a toxicology study with over a thousandfold margin of intake compared with projected human consumption, and by showing that this protein is, as expected, rapidly degraded under conditions simulating human digestion. In addition, this protein was shown to share no similarities to known allergens or toxins. The totality of information allowed the conclusion that this protein posed no significant toxicologic or allergenic concerns for human or animal consumption. This kind of safety assessment is typical of the assessments done for crops developed through biotechnology.

One concern that has frequently been raised about foods derived through biotechnology is that an allergenic protein could be inserted into a food, thereby making that food allergenic to consumers without their realizing it. Developers of such products take several steps to assure that allergens are not inadvertently inserted into foods. First, the amino acid sequence of the inserted protein is compared against a database containing the amino acid sequences of known allergens. If there are no matches in sequences of amino acids known to be responsible for eliciting the immunologic response, then it is probable the inserted protein will not be allergenic. Further studies, nevertheless, are conducted to confirm that the inserted protein is not allergenic and will be rapidly digested by gastric juices.

> *Biotechnology clearly has tremendous potential for revolutionizing agriculture.*

More recently, crops are being genetically modified to intentionally be different (e.g., not substantially equivalent in composition) compared with its parent. For example, canola has been genetically modified to have certain enzymes that greatly increase its content of carotenoids compared with its parent. In this situation, it is important to show not only that the expressed enzymes are safe, but also that the increased levels of carotenoids and any other changes resulting from the increased production of carotenoids also are safe.

Genetically modified foods are ecologically safe

Manufacturers wishing to introduce a new genetically modified food to the market spend several years developing data to support safety of the product. In addition to developing the extensive compositional information described above, manufacturers also must show the safety of their products for the environment. The transformed seeds must be grown and tested first in greenhouses and then in field trials to make sure the new plant does not have unfavorable agronomic traits and does not pose any significant environmental or ecologic concerns. This includes assessment for weediness, competitiveness, safety to nontarget organisms, disease susceptibility, and other agronomic and ecologic characteristics. If the crop of interest cross-pollinates with other crops or weeds, the impact of such cross-pollination is also assessed. For crops genetically enhanced for protection against insects or disease, the specificity of the encoded protein and its safety to nontarget insects, mammals, birds, fish, and other nontarget organisms are evaluated in detail.

Finally, the genetically modified plants can be crossed with numerous varieties of traditional plants to achieve an array of new seeds containing the genetically modified trait. These and other data are shared with regulatory scientists at the United States Department of Agriculture (USDA) and Environmental Protection Agency (EPA) as needed throughout the development process. The USDA and EPA require formal premarket approvals for each product that they have jurisdiction over (USDA for all genetically modified plants and EPA for pesticide-containing plants). Although the final regulatory process for biotechnology-derived crops in the United States involves a voluntary consultation with the FDA, every product introduced in the United States has gone through this consultation with the FDA. This consultation process is considered de facto mandatory by the developers of these products, because the farmers and food industry would not grow or use a product that had not completed this process. The FDA is currently reconsidering whether this process should remain voluntary or be made mandatory.

International safety assessments

In addition to the US FDA, international scientific and regulatory organizations also have established systems to assure the safety of foods derived from biotechnology. For example, the Organization for Economic Cooperation and Development, the World Health Organization, the International Life Sciences Institute, and the Food and Agriculture Organization have convened international experts to discuss, evaluate, and make recommendations regarding the safety of these products. Their conclusions are consistent with those of the FDA: foods developed through biotechnology are not inherently less safe than foods developed through traditional techniques. Biotechnology merely broadens the genetic range of traits that are introduced into food crops. In situations in which biotechnology produces a difference in the new product versus the parent, the safety assessment should focus on this difference.

In Europe, the safety of genetically modified foods is evaluated under the Novel Foods and Food Ingredients Regulation. As in the United States, this regulation requires that before a novel food is marketed, manufacturers must document that the new food does not present a safety or nutritional risk. The environmental impact of genetically improved crops, including potential issues such as insect resistance management, safety to nontarget organisms, and the consequences of cross-pollination with related species, are also formally considered.

The effectiveness of the safety evaluation process is perhaps best illustrated by the case of a soybean in which a gene from the Brazil nut was introduced to improve its nutritional quality. Because nuts are known to contain allergenic proteins, immunologic studies were recommended to determine whether any Brazil nut allergens had been transferred to the soybean. In fact, the soybean was found to contain an allergenic Brazil nut protein; development of the product ceased, and the soybean variety was not commercialized. This example illustrates that the safety evaluation process and regulatory system are effective in identifying and discontinuing the development of products that could pose risks to consumers. Before biotechnology-derived products are commercialized, the protein(s) produced from the inserted gene(s) must be shown not to increase the allergenicity of food products derived from these plants.

To illustrate the extent of regulatory and scientific review of plant biotechnology products, 27 different regulatory agencies reviewed the safety of soybeans modified to be tolerant to glyphosate. These soybeans are approved (for either production or consumption or both) in 13 different countries around the world. In addition, numerous scientific articles summarizing the data generated to assess the food, feed, and environmental safety of this product have been published in peer-reviewed journals.

The tremendous potential of agricultural biotechnology

Biotechnology clearly has tremendous potential for revolutionizing agriculture, food production, world nutrition, and health. With an ever-increasing population and shrinking natural resources, the benefits of increasing food production without unduly stressing the environment cannot be overstated. Improvements in food quality, availability, and nutritional enhancements are equally important. However, as with any new application of technology, it is necessary to evaluate potential health risks. Safety experts and regulatory agencies worldwide have designed science-based frameworks and safety assessment approaches for the food, feed, and environmental safety evaluation of genetically modified food crops. Several crops with favorable agronomic traits have cleared these evaluations, and others with nutritional and quality enhancements are expected to be available over the next several years. The public has welcomed some applications of biotechnology, particularly in medicine. Public reaction to plant biotechnology in food production has been mixed. Part of the difficulty has been the lack of information and understanding of what biotechnology is, its risks and benefits, and the regulatory systems in place to assure food safety. Increased knowledge about biotechnology will permit consumers to make informed decisions about foods derived from this technology.

6

Agricultural Biotechnology Companies Sacrifice the Environment for Economic Gain

Sonja A. Schmitz

Sonja A. Schmitz is a doctoral candidate in plant systematics and evolution at the University of Vermont and a former employee of DuPont Corporation, where she worked as a molecular biologist in its agricultural biotechnology department.

The decisions businesses make about the development of agricultural biotechnology are motivated by their desire for profit at the expense of the environment. Cross-pollination and the spread of herbicide-resistant genes to neighboring conventional crops could create a serious ecological threat to surrounding areas and wild plants. Furthermore, genetically engineered crops produce herbicide-resistant weeds, which only serves to create opportunities for large biotechnology companies to sell more of their products. Society readily believes that technology will find answers to the kinds of environmental problems caused by agricultural biotechnology. However, the biotechnology industry is not motivated to find the best solutions to such problems. Its motivation is the generation of capital. Agricultural biotechnology should not be driven by commercial interests, but by what is most important for the world's ecological safety.

G old beads blast from the barrel of a gun at 1,000 m.p.h. Their target: soft plant tissue nestled in a sterile Petri dish. The golden bullets blast their way through thick cell walls, membranes and cytoplasm of the plant cells. Finally, they penetrate the nuclear membrane and deliver the information with which they have been coated; cloned genes that insert themselves randomly along the chromosomes. Only a fraction of the cells will survive the bombardment. Only one in a million will express the new genetic information correctly. That cell will be grown to maturity and eventually, after years of nurturing in the hands of plant breeders, will produce fields of genetically engineered plants. Vandana Shiva, director of the Research Foundation for Science, Technology and Natural Resource Policy in India, describes the genetic engineering of plants as the latest manifestation of colonization: this time, invasion of the seed. The process of colonization uses weapons in order to exploit another culture. The gene gun, known as Bioblaster, is the weapon of biotechnology. To many scientists it represents a technological advance that will revolutionize agriculture.

> *Agricultural biotechnology is producing commodities whose sole purpose is to profit the industry that makes them.*

In recent years, up to 50 million acres of genetically engineered crops have been planted on US farmland. Genetically engineered foods are for sale at the supermarket. To the agricultural industry these events herald a revolution in biotechnology. The public is concerned about use of genetically engineered organisms in agriculture because of the incompatibility of biotechnology with sustainable agriculture, the environmental impacts of releasing engineered organisms, and the safety of genetically engineered foods, among other issues. In drafting organic standards for the US Department of Agriculture (USDA), the question arose as to whether engineered foods should be considered organic. Nearly 300,000 people wrote letters and postcards to the USDA, largely in response to the suggestion that genetically engineered products might qualify as organic.

These issues are important. They are also difficult to resolve because they require going beyond the facts of science to debate ethics and values. Such a debate impinges on issues of democracy, the access to technology, and its effect on social structure and community. It requires us to have agency and agree upon a vision for the future. Currently, decisions surrounding the use of technology are driven primarily by economics and the corporations that dominate the market. Agricultural biotechnology is promoted as a sustainable means of addressing the issues of food security and safety, but, in fact, biotechnology is generating products whose sole purpose is to benefit and sustain industrial agriculture. . . .

Disillusionment with the biotech industry

When I graduated in the late 1980s with a Master's degree in molecular biology, biotechnology was an industry in its infancy. . . . Feeling proud of my educational accomplishment and hopeful that as a scientist I could make a valuable contribution to society, I accepted a lucrative offer from DuPont and began working as a molecular biologist in their agricultural biotechnology department. During my employment there, I worked for many good people and dedicated scientists. I learned that agriculture was no longer synonymous with the notion of the small family farm. Small to medium-size farms were quickly being replaced by industrial farms, and companies like DuPont played an important role in this transition.

Job satisfaction became an issue when I realized the projects on which I worked did not address food security or safety. For instance, there was the "novel starch" project: genetically engineering corn to produce altered starches. Although scientifically challenging, the end product was destined for the food processors who fill grocery shelves with such items as instant puddings, gravies and frozen dinners. Then there were the "fartless" soybeans, a project we jokingly called cloning the "FART 1" gene. These soybeans contained smaller amounts of the sugars which normally result in human flatulence. My colleagues were working on equally "socially beneficial" projects. How was this work part of the agricultural revolution that biotechnology was supposed to spur?

My ever-growing disillusionment culminated in the realization that biotechnology is big business. This issue gets lost in the debate between an industry that tells us we need their technology to ensure abundant, safe and nutritious food, and activists who focus on the health and environmental risks. At the core of the industry's argument for developing biotechnologies is the forever impending human population boom and the growing demand for more food. Some activists are quick to point out that food security is more an issue of political economy than productivity. There is sufficient food produced globally; it just doesn't get to everyone because of political and economic inequities.

Agricultural biotechnology is producing commodities whose sole purpose is to profit the industry that makes them. These new products do not address the social problems of hunger, nutrition, environmental safety and health to which they make claim. Aside from our recently acquired capacity to clone genes and transfer them between unrelated species, agricultural biotechnology is not generating anything unique or new. I no longer believe that the use of biotechnology heralds the dawn of an agricultural revolution.

The value of food products

"Value-added" is a value-laden term. It is one of several buzz words adorning the overheads of corporate presentations. Whether they are called value-added, value-enhanced, identity-preserved or specialty grains, the terms refer to fruits and vegetables that (1) are designed for delayed ripening; (2) are engineered for increased yields of the starch, protein, fibre or oil extracted from them; or (3) contain genetically altered starch, oils or protein.

Value-added grains are not new to agriculture; they have existed since the 1930s when plant breeding produced high-yielding varieties of hybrid corn. Many of today's specialty grains, like corn seed that contains 8 per cent oil instead of the standard 4 per cent, are produced through plant breeding. The latest value-added grains are the result of genetic engineering: canola (oil-seed rape) that has elevated levels of unsaturated fats, or corn that may contain essential amino acids. Several biotech companies are developing "novel" starches. A closer look at starch technology allows us to examine the role that biotechnology plays in generating products that are questionably "novel."

Starches are extracted from a variety of different crops including corn, rice, wheat and potatoes. Each starch behaves differently during the cooking process, resulting in a variety of thicknesses that add texture to our food. Anyone who cooks knows that starch can be used "as is" to thicken soups, gravies and puddings. The food industry, however, is interested in adding functional properties to foods by chemically altering starch: food labelled with "modified starch" as one of its ingredients is made with a chemically modified starch. For example, many of the fat-free products on the market today are the result of replacing fats and oils with a chemically modified corn starch that creates the "mouth feel" of fats.

> *// Who should bear responsibility for the ecological risks posed by genetically engineered plants in the environment? //*

Current research efforts are aimed at developing "novel" starches through genetic engineering. For biotechnologists, this means experimenting with the pathways for starch metabolism in an effort to produce a "naturally" modified starch that behaves like a chemically modified starch. There is a fascination in exploring the relationships among enzymes to see how manipulating their genes can alter the structure of starch. They seek to replace chemically modified starches with genetically engineered ones, provided of course that instant pudding still looks and feels like instant pudding. The "typical" consumer will never know the difference between pie filling made with genetically altered starch and one that is chemically modified. What is so novel about that?

Herbicide-tolerant crops

Herbicide-tolerant crops (HTCs) are another commodity produced by the so-called revolution in agricultural biotechnology. Unlike genetically engineered foods whose primary value to the industry is in cost savings, HTCs add profitability by creating a new market niche. HTCs and their corresponding herbicides are sold together as treatment systems and are marketed as sustainable, environmentally friendly additions to chemical agriculture. Monsanto's Roundup Ready soybeans and Aventis/AgroEvo's Liberty Link corn were among the first to reach the market. While the industry claims environmental benefits from the use of HTCs, the problems created by their use, especially the emergence of herbicide-resistant weeds and the transfer of genes to wild relatives of crops, invite just the kinds of solutions the chemical industry is eager to solve.

The industry cannot guarantee that HTCs will reduce the application of herbicide to farmland. Their careful use of qualifiers such as "has the potential to . . ." and "may lower the use of . . ." in their propaganda suggests doubt. Critics point out that rapid degradation of herbicide could result in the need to apply herbicide more often, as weeds emerge after it degrades. Also, since these herbicides are sprayed directly onto crops, as opposed to direct soil application, they are more likely to drift onto neighbouring fields. This could induce other farmers to switch to the same herbicide to protect their crops, thereby increasing overall herbicide use.

> *Technology is directly related to generating capital. It has become a mechanism for generating new markets and commodities.*

HTCs do not exclude the use of other herbicides. A herbicide treatment regimen typically requires several applications of several different herbicides to combat all weeds. Although broad-spectrum herbicides eliminate most weeds, they are not effective on all of them. For instance, Liberty, a broad-spectrum herbicide sold by Aventis/AgroEvo, is not effective on the roots and rhizomes of quack and Johnson grasses. Therefore farmers who plant Liberty Link corn and apply Liberty herbicide have to purchase additional herbicides to control these weeds.

Herbicide-resistant weeds

Organisms have a natural compulsion to overcome barriers that stand in the way of survival. From bacteria to plants, organisms develop resistances after repeated exposure to deleterious substances whether they be antibiotics, viruses or herbicides. The emergence of herbicide-resistant weeds has plagued agriculture for decades. [Since 1991] the number of weed populations resistant to an array of herbicides has increased. Whether herbicide-resistant weeds emerge spontaneously or are the result of genetic engineering, the transference of resistance genes to neighbouring populations of the same species is a matter of environmental concern. More research needs to be done to assess adequately the impact of unwanted herbicide-resistant plants on surrounding habitats. The industry's response to the emergence of herbicide-resistant weeds is to implement an integrated weed management programme. This entails rotating HTCs and herbicides. For example, if Roundup-resistant soybeans are grown one year, they should be rotated with Liberty Link corn the following year. They remain silent on the issue of gene flow to natural populations.

> *It is naive to believe that the agricultural industry will create solutions that are environmentally sustainable.*

Who should bear responsibility for the ecological risks posed by genetically engineered plants in the environment? Federal officials at the USDA believe that because chemical companies have an incentive to protect their investments, they will naturally bear the responsibility. Companies risk losing a portion of the herbicide market if resistance genes are transferred to wild relatives because it renders the herbicide obsolete. But, consider this: if new weeds are created by the transfer of herbicide-resistant genes, it forces the farmer to purchase other herbicides. The chemical companies can rely on the sale of traditional herbicides or offer the farmer a different seed/herbicide system for purchase. Why else would Monsanto and other companies invest billions of dollars in research that would appear to lose money eventually? The agricultural chemical companies have an army of chemists constantly developing new herbicides and just as many molecular biologists probing the metabolism of crop plants for genes that will confer resistance. The problems posed by the introduction of seed/herbicide systems only serve to invite another technological fix. Herbicide technology, whether "traditional" or genetically engineered, has a built-in obsolescence. Seed/herbicide systems are the logical solution for companies who operate in a system that depends upon technological fixes to keep generating new markets.

Biotechnology's built-in obsolescence

Beginning with the scientific revolution of the seventeenth century, we have increasingly sought answers through science and technology. There is now a pervasive belief that solutions to our technological problems lie in generating new technologies. We have become so enamoured of science that it is difficult to recognize its limitations and distinguish between its real economic power and the illusion of its power to provide sustainable solutions. This illusion protects us from confronting the more difficult issues that underlie the social problems science pretends to address. It is perhaps useful to remind ourselves that science is an art, a palette of techniques, in our relentless quest to understand our place in nature. It is much easier (and more fun!) to go into the lab and clone a gene than it is to tackle the social and economic restructuring required to create a society that is in sustainable harmony with the planet.

Our love affair with science and technology is not the only reason we maintain faith in their power to provide answers. Technology is directly related to generating capital. It has become a mechanism for generating new markets and commodities. While technology creates many modern innovations, it does not always represent the best solution, particularly in agriculture. Western economies have historically relied upon a built-in obsolescence to their products while maintaining the ability to create replacements. That is why companies have research and development departments. Biotechnology fits this agenda by generating products that will, for example, replace chemically modified foods with genetically engineered ones and by adding herbicide-resistant crops to their product lines.

> *The application of technology should be determined by the needs of an ecological society, as opposed to the needs of a market economy.*

Genetically engineered products are sold as the progeny of an agricultural revolution that will improve the quality, nutrition and abundance of our food supply. At best, the notion of an "agricultural revolution" reflects a social ignorance and arrogance that is typical of the scientific community. At worst, it is an intentional lie generated by an industry trying to promote itself. The insidiousness of these products lies in their role as technological fixes. When markets become saturated, as with chemically modified food starches, or problems arise, such as weed resistance to herbicides, new commodities must be created in order to realize profit. Scientists employed in research and development are under continual pressure to create new products or design technologies to decrease production and processing costs. Given the market pressure to produce new commodities, it is naive to believe that the agricultural industry will create solutions that are environmentally sustainable. When they use the term "sustainable" they mean able to sustain their share of the market economy.

Ecological society vs. market economy

Our current economic system is incompatible with an ecological society, one that can sustain itself within the environmental limits of our planet. Sustainable agriculture, when defined as regenerative, low-input, diversified, and decentralized, is the antithesis of industrial agriculture. Industrial agriculture depends upon obsolescence, high inputs, monocultures, and the centralization of power. While not yet a monopoly, industrial agriculture is increasingly controlled by just a few companies. Such centralization of power threatens democracy. We live in an era where the meaning of democracy has been diminished. The majority of us have lost the power to make decisions about issues that impact on our communities and environment. In order to live in ecological harmony within the limits of our environment, we must recreate an egalitarian, political forum for making decisions.

At a lecture given by [noted environmentalist] Vandana Shiva, I asked which she perceived as the more imminent danger: the potential environmental and health risks of releasing genetically engineered organisms, or the insidious role the products of biotechnology play in promoting the growth of capitalism. She replied that while the two should not be separated, potential environmental risks may not be fully realized for another ten or fifteen years, but the social and economic effects of globalization are affecting peoples' lives today, particularly in developing countries where agribusiness strategies, including intellectual property rights over genetically engineered crops, threaten to devastate indigenous farmers. It is important to expose the role of agricultural biotechnology as another technological fix rather than a method that will revolutionize agriculture.

For those of us who work to create an ecological society, it is important to understand the role science and technology play. Only then can we begin to address the larger questions about what role we want technology and science to play in an ecological society. Would we choose to use biotechnologies if they were divorced from their role in sustaining the chemical agriculture industry? The application of technology should be determined by the needs of an ecological society, as opposed to the needs of a market economy, an economy on a collision course with environmental disaster.

7

Cloning Humans Is Ethical

Ronald M. Green

Ronald M. Green is a professor for the study of ethics and human values at Dartmouth College. He is also the chair of Dartmouth's Department of Religion as well as chair of the ethics advisory board for Advanced Cell Technology, Inc. He has written numerous articles and books about ethics, including The Human Embryo Research Debates: Bioethics in the Vortex of Controversy. *Green also has served as director of the Office of Genome Ethics for the National Human Genome Research Institute.*

Human cloning has great potential benefits, but many people have panicked over exaggerated reports on the dangers of this emerging technology. In the public debates on cloning, participants have tended to present nightmare scenarios without examining their likelihood or magnitude. Moreover, the physical and psychological risks to the cloned child are often distorted. To date no one has shown that any of these risks are great enough to warrant a ban on cloning. The recommendation by the National Bioethics Advisory Commission for a federal ban on human cloning research could lead the best scientists to avoid the field and leave cloning research to irresponsible scientists on the fringes of the profession. Despite all the overblown fears about cloning, it is a technology that can be used in an ethical way to improve people's lives.

I begin this discussion with the conviction that 10 or 20 years from now around the world a modest number of children

Ronald M. Green, "Much Ado About Mutton: An Ethical Review of the Cloning Controversy," *Cloning and the Future of Human Embryo Research*, edited by Paul Lauritzen. New York: Oxford University Press, 2001. Copyright © 2001 by Paul Lauritzen. All rights reserved. Reproduced by permission of the publisher.

(several hundred to several thousand) will be born each year as a result of somatic cell nuclear transfer (SCNT) cloning. I further assume that within the same period cloning will have come to be looked on as just one more available technique of assisted reproduction among the many in use: in vitro fertilization (IVF), egg and sperm donation, intracytoplasmic sperm injection, surrogacy. I hope to show why this outcome is both predictable and ethically acceptable.

Exploring the patterns of moral reasoning

Against this background, however, I also want to explore why, at a certain moment in the 1990s, the prospect of human cloning created so much controversy around the world and led many people to want it banned. My exploration of this question will not primarily be at the level of cultural analysis. Obviously, many identifiable cultural phenomena contributed to this emotional reaction—from popular fiction and films to broad anxieties generated by changing family patterns and rapid advances in the life sciences. These cultural factors lent energy to the controversy, and they merit study in their own right. Nevertheless, what I want to focus on are the patterns of moral reasoning that led so many people to oppose cloning. What the cloning controversy tells us, I think, is that there are ways of thinking about new biomedical technologies that tend to cast them in a very negative light. It is worthwhile to identify these patterns as we enter an era of accelerating advances in the life sciences.

I also want to show how some of these patterns of reasoning evidenced themselves in the report of the National Bioethics Advisory Committee (NBAC), *Cloning Human Beings*. Issued at the outset of the cloning controversy, this report is in many ways a balanced document that seeks to calm fears and place the issue of cloning in an informed and reasoned context. At the same time, however, the NBAC's approach to the cloning issue reflects some of the patterns of reasoning that contributed during this period to widespread rejection of this innovative technology.

Cloning is advantageous in many situations

I have said that I think cloning will eventually be an accepted—and morally acceptable—reproductive technology. Let me begin by indicating why I believe this is so in order to establish a framework against which we can measure the concerns of those holding a different view. The most likely use of cloning will be circumstances in which one or both members of a couple do not produce the gametes (eggs or sperm) needed for sexual reproduction but wish a child with some genetic relation to his or her parents. Couples in which the male partner has undergone bilateral orchiectomy (complete castration) or otherwise lacks viable sperm are one example. If such couples wish to have a genetic connection with their offspring, they can currently resort to sperm donation, with the result that the child will share half of his or her genetic material with the mother and none with the father. Because sperm donation introduces a third party into the relationship and raises complex questions about the child's future relation to his or her biological father, some couples in this position may reasonably prefer to have a cloned child who has all the genetic material of either the mother or the father. Somatic cell nuclear transfer cloning will make this possible. For similar reasons, lesbian couples will also find cloning an attractive alternative, permitting each member of the pair to bear a child with her partner's genotype. Sperm donation is an option here, but some lesbian couples do not wish to involve third parties in their reproductive lives.

> *There are good reasons, not all of which will be equally compelling to everyone, why cloning may be both desirable and allowed.*

It has been said that cloning may prove attractive to couples each of whose members bears a serious recessive genetic disorder. I am not personally persuaded that this is true. The evolving technology of preimplantation genetic diagnosis (PGD) can provide such couples an alternative by permitting clinicians to create a number of embryos, test them to distinguish those that merely carry the disorder from those that will be affected by it, and then transfer only those embryos likely to be healthy. It is true, however, that the existence of multiple—and in some cases unknown—mutations may frustrate these efforts and render cloning a preferred approach for some people.

In any case, some individuals who have experienced the birth of a child with a serious genetic disease may be assumed to wish to avoid the "lottery" of sexual reproduction altogether in the future. Cloning is one way they can do this.

> *Perhaps the most obvious feature of the early cloning debate was the prevalence of nightmare scenarios.*

It may be objected here that all these scenarios privilege people's wish to have genetically related children. In a world of burgeoning populations where so many children are currently living in foster homes or orphanages, do we really want to encourage these questionable new forms of parenting? I could reply to these objections in many ways. Assisted reproductive technologies make little or no significant contribution to the growth in world population (which is largely occurring in underdeveloped countries where these technologies are not used). More important, these objections do not apply exclusively to cloning. They arise in connection with any of the established reproductive technologies and are not usually considered a reason for prohibiting access to them. In any case, my aim here is not to evaluate all the arguments pro and con for permitting infertile people, lesbians, or others in similar circumstances to have children via cloning. I merely want to indicate that there are good reasons, not all of which will be equally compelling to everyone, why cloning may be both desirable and allowed. We currently have a wide array of assisted reproductive technologies (ARTs) to help couples with reproductive problems. Cloning, I believe, will soon be regarded as merely another one of them.

Cloning is also likely to be the principal instrument of future gene therapy. Many serious genetic disorders have their start during the period of embryonic and fetal development. If we are to prevent or correct them by gene therapy, we must intervene early. The technical challenge is to insert a corrected gene into every cell of a developing embryo, something that is very difficult using most viral or other gene vectors, which penetrate only one out of hundreds or thousands of cells. This problem can be overcome by means of cloning. Researchers can introduce the vector into a large population of differenti-ated cells gathered from adult or embryo donors. They can test to identify those few cells where the gene becomes properly in-serted into the nuclear DNA. Using the nucleus of such a cell, they can then perform a cloning procedure to produce an em-bryo that, as it grows, possesses the corrected gene in every cell of its body. With the Human Genome Project greatly expand-ing our knowledge of the genetic basis of diseases, there will be increasing numbers of people who will want to intervene at the genetic level early in life. Cloning may be widely used in this connection.

Questionable patterns of moral reasoning

From its start, the cloning issue has been approached with a se-ries of concerns, questions, and standards for evaluation that made negative conclusions about it almost inevitable. In this part of my discussion, I want to itemize those approaches and compare them, as necessary, with less forbidding standards ap-plied to other, widely accepted areas of biomedical practice and innovation.

Nightmare scenarios in the cloning debate

Perhaps the most obvious feature of the early cloning debate was the prevalence of nightmare scenarios with little or no ba-sis in facts or technical possibilities. Fictional literature and pop-ular films fed some of these scenarios; others were based on an unreasonable and uninformed estimate of what cloning tech-nology involves or the role of genes in human development.

One such vision may partly explain the immediate impulse to political (and even presidential) involvement in the cloning debate. It is the specter that cloning will be used by a tyrannical regime to mass-produce an army of superwarriors. Against a background of Nazi breeding experiments, popular films like *The Boys From Brazil*, and very prevalent fears of [former Iraqi dicta-tor] Saddam Hussein's development of biological weaponry, these visions were understandable, but not in any way justified. Lurking here was the serious misconception that cloning can make possible the industrial-scale manufacture of desired hu-man genotypes, bypassing pregnancy and years of childrearing. In reality, if Saddam Hussein were to embark on this route as a means of conquest, his program would require the reproductive enslavement of tens of thousands of women, and he would have to wait 20 years to see the results of his efforts. In addition, if Hussein really were committed to this idea, he could accomplish the same end by means of old-fashioned sexual reproduction using selected male and female breeders or their gametes—as in the Nazi Lebensborn program more than half a century ago. Because genotype is not phenotype—a theme I will return to shortly—there is also a high likelihood that many of Saddam's cloned warriors would no more exhibit his desired traits than would selected sexually reproduced children or even a well-trained population of normal recruits. . . .

Commercialized reproduction

Another prevalent nightmare scenario during this period was the vision of sexual reproduction being replaced by new commercialized reproduction revolving around the sale of proven or desired genotypes. The vision of thousands of Cindy Crawfords, Brad Pitts, or Michael Jordans danced frighteningly before some critics' eyes. These concerns were fed by the prompt appearance of spurious websites offering cloned copies of celebrities (one even promised an instant Elvis). Unlike the fear of cloned warriors, the problem here was not misinformation. Commercialized mass reproduction like this is technically possible. Furthermore, because a clone can be produced from virtually any intact diploid body cell—one derived from a blood spot or even a hair follicle—cloning poses novel problems in terms of reproductive privacy and the unconsented use of one's genome by other people. Were this reproductive scenario to come to pass, doctors, dentists, hairdressers, and others with access to celebrities' DNA might have to sign agreements not to use it for personal gain.

These worries about commercialized genotypes betray not technical ignorance but an interesting and, to some extent, self-contradictory assessment of human beings' reproductive desires. On the one hand, many who oppose cloning criticize what they regarded as an obsessive concern with the perpetuation of one's genotype. On the other hand, some of these critics also seem to believe that many parents will gladly forego sexual reproduction—and hence the perpetuation of their genotypes—in order to have a celebrity child. In fact, there is substantial evidence that people, even those suffering from infertility who must use donor gametes, basically want to have children like themselves. The "Nobel Prize–Winners" sperm bank opened some years ago by Linus Pauling has done little business. Couples using donor gametes frequently select a sperm or egg donor with desirable qualities like evidence of advanced education or physical attractiveness. As Teri Royal, director of one of the nation's largest fertility registries, observes, however, these couples typically want a child whose intelligence is comparable with their own and with whom they'll be able to relate. "They're not looking for any Mensa [a society of people with high IQs] applicant," she says.

The fear that people will readily abandon normal parenting and reproductive patterns points to a deeper problem in the moral reasoning of many who strongly oppose human cloning: their fundamental mistrust of natural human inclinations. We often encounter new technological or social developments that seem to threaten widely accepted forms of sexual expression, parenting, or family relations. In responding to these perceived threats, it is always important to respect the power and persistence of normal human drives and to resist the impulse to overreact to new developments in repressive ways. After all, if heterosexual sexual expression and familial affection are important enough to fear their loss, they are also not likely to be massively abandoned when confronted by alternate modes of behavior. Those afraid that cloning might lead people to relinquish sexual reproduction commit the same error in reasoning as homophobic people who fear that tolerance of homosexuality will lead to a mass exodus from heterosexuality. Both fail to trust in the force of the values that they are seeking to defend.

Concerns of risks associated with cloning

The bulk of informed critical opinion about human cloning has been focused not on nightmare scenarios but on possible risks to the children born as a result of cloning procedures. These risks are either physical or psychological. Because human cloning has never been accomplished, many of these harms are speculative in nature. This is not itself a count against them, because caution is always in order when possibly significant risks are involved. Nevertheless, the highly speculative nature of these discussions points to a larger problem in this debate. As we will see, cloning critics have frequently invoked standards of caution and non-injury for this technology that have not been—and probably should not be—applied to other biomedical or reproductive innovations. In addition, the debate has frequently been framed as though the only questions of importance are those about risk to prospective children. Other interests and considerations, especially those of parents, are often omitted from consideration. The result is an evaluation process that has the tendency to lead toward negative conclusions because no substantial values are advanced on the other side.

There is an important lesson here. It is easy to exaggerate the risks of technological innovations. Quite apart from the ease of constructing catastrophic "worst case" scenarios when unknown risks are multiplied by unknown risks, change itself is often perceived as dangerous because it threatens known and established values. The benefits of technological innovations, however, are often less obvious because what is unknown cannot be assessed. . . .

> *There is an important lesson here. It is easy to exaggerate the risks of technological innovations.*

I will indicate some of the ways that these misleading patterns of reasoning evidence themselves in some assessments of cloning's risks. First, however, I must state emphatically that concern about the harmful effects of cloning on the children produced by this technology is completely appropriate. I need to do this because two positions sometimes advanced in this context hold otherwise. One is the view that no person can be harmed by cloning because it involves human embryos, which are not regarded as juridical human beings in United States law (and in many people's ethical views). What is at stake in the cloning debate, however, are not embryos but future born children. Even though they may not be in existence when a cloning procedure is begun, children produced by cloning can be adversely affected by it. It is well established in ethics and law that children who are born alive can recover damages for prenatal injury done to them. The same applies to harm done through cloning.

A second view denying the possibility of harming children through cloning is based on the writings of [philosophers] Derek Parfit, David Heyd, and others. In the cloning debate,

University of Texas Law School professor John Robertson has most frequently voiced it. According to this view, judgments of harm always involve the comparison of an individual's condition *ex ante* (before the alleged injury was done) with the individual's condition *post ante* (following the alleged injury). Harm is done if someone is made worse off as a result of another's actions. Robertson acknowledges that cloning may cause some very serious physical and psychological injuries to children. Because none of these children would have been conceived without use of the cloning procedure, however, we cannot say that they have been made "worse off" by it. Sustaining this claim, says Robertson, would involve showing that the child's life is of such low quality that it would have been better off if it had never come into being at all. Because even individuals born with serious ailments and disabilities are usually glad to be alive, however, it cannot be said that a cloned child would have preferred never to live. Researchers, clinicians, or parents will clearly harm a child by cloning only in rare cases where the child's suffering is so great that most individuals with the same problems would rationally prefer to die. . . .

Despite Robertson's or others' contentions, the instinct to assess cloning in terms of possible harms to the child is sound. This leaves unaddressed, however, the question of whether any of the speculative or real harms are sufficiently grave to lead us to conclude that human cloning should not be attempted. In approaching this issue it is useful to distinguish between physical and psychological harms because the former are somewhat more concrete. What I want to suggest now is that, in most discussions of the ethics of cloning, no one has shown that harms in either of these areas are likely to be so great as to lead us to want to ban cloning research or its most likely clinical applications.

Possible physical harms to the child

Even if it were technically possible, it certainly would not have been reasonable to try to clone a human being in the period following the announcement of Dolly. A fundamental principle of human subjects research is that appropriate studies using animals, preferably of closely related species, should first be undertaken to determine the safety and efficacy of procedures before they are applied to human beings. No one has yet accomplished this for human cloning. Furthermore, initial human research will have to be done with embryos not intended for transfer, as was true in the case of IVF [in vitro fertilization] research in the 1960s and 1970s. (I will return to this point when I look more closely at the NBAC's report.) Only once animals evidencing no anomalies have been born and lived a normal life span and a series of viable and apparently healthy human embryos have been produced can researchers offer fully informed and freely consenting parents the opportunity to participate in further research by attempting a live birth.

> *Because cloning can benefit people, the aim is to permit people to use it while eliminating those aspects of it that lead directly to harm.*

A critical question is what the precise baseline of possible harm to the child should be. . . . I think that in terms of health we must strive to give a child a start in life roughly equivalent to others in its birth cohort. This reflects our interest in discouraging behaviors leading to suffering on the child's part or creating significant additional burdens for the child's parents or society. As one possible measure of this, we can say that a child is harmed when he or she is deliberately or knowingly brought into being with health problems or disabilities serious enough to warrant a malpractice suit in the context of obstetrical or pediatric medicine.

Elevated risks are acceptable

When new reproductive technologies are involved, however, this does not necessarily mean a risk standard equivalent to that of normal conception and birth. As has been true with the introduction of IVF, assisted hatching, intracytoplasmic sperm injection, and other new reproductive technologies, a somewhat elevated risk level for the child above the baseline of unassisted reproduction might be permissible. The reason for this is not, as Robertson believes, because harm to the child is offset by the benefit to it of being born. No such benefit exists. Rather, it is the benefit to the child's otherwise infertile parents that justifies this small increment of risk. When one has experienced infertility, the desire to have a child is legitimate and pressing. In other areas, parents' wishes are commonly regarded as justifying modest increments of risk of harm to their children. (For example, even though the risks of birth defects are somewhat higher in such cases, we sympathize with couples who marry late and who try to start a family.) Because parents will bear many of the emotional and financial costs of a child's congenital problems, they should also have a right, within reasonable limits, to accept these small increments of risk for their child.

Confine risk assessments to the child

Before leaving the matter of physical harms, I must note that risk assessments for cloning research should stay focused on risks to the child to be: not on gametes or embryos. During the initial debates surrounding cloning, commentators reported that 277 attempts had been made to clone Dolly. Many people naturally assumed that this would be a morally unacceptable loss rate if human subjects were involved. These numbers are, however, misleading. Most of this loss took place in the initial efforts to achieve cell division to the [early embryo] blastocyst stage following nuclear transfer. These failures represent a massive loss of oocytes and somatic cell nuclei that, at least until there is some technical innovation in the source of ova, will have to be remedied if human cloning is ever to be efficient and cost effective. The loss of oocytes and somatic cell nuclei does not, however, represent a moral problem. Neither egg cells nor body cells have a moral claim on us. The final number of blastocyst-stage embryos produced was 29, of which 13 were judged viable for transfer. One lamb, Dolly, resulted. If this were human research and the high loss rate did not indicate an elevated congenital risk for the resulting child, these numbers would pose no significant moral problem. A high ratio of transferred embryos to births is already common in current human IVF procedures. Only those who regard the early embryo as morally equivalent to a child will be troubled by this rate of loss.

The stir about these numbers is important, however, because it highlights two recurring features of the cloning controversy. One is the poor quality of much press coverage and reporters' tendency to emphasize seemingly disturbing news. The other is the constant presence in these reproductive debates of emotional energy drawn from our abortion controversies. Properly understood, the ratio 276 to 1 points to nothing more than the rudimentary state of cloning technology. For some who view the early human embryo as sacrosanct, however, this ratio represents a potentially catastrophic loss of human life and confirms their fears that cloning will lead to the massive abuse of human beings. These worries may be legitimate, of course, but they should not be wrongly intensified by a particular—and I think erroneous—moral estimate of the early embryo.

Possible psychological harms

In many discussions of cloning, the risk of physical damage captured less attention than a host of possible psychological harms for the child. Underlying these concerns is a novel feature of cloning, especially somatic cell cloning: the possibility of replicating in an infant the genotype of someone who is already alive or has lived before. The principal worry is that the cloned child would be exposed to acute, and ultimately oppressive, expectations for its development. A child brought into being with the genes of a successful parent, an outstanding athlete, or a prima ballerina might be harmed in several ways. Parental expectations may force the child into intensive programs of training or into career directions that do not correspond to the child's real interests. Failure to live up to the expectations established by the genotype donor might cause the child to experience reduced self-esteem. Parents might emotionally distance themselves from a cloned child they regarded as having failed to live up to his or her promise. [Australian bioethicist] Peter Singer, for example, asks whether parents of offspring produced by cloning "would be able to love their children with the uncritical love of parents who love their children for what they are."

> *Instead of inviting the best scientists to assume responsibility for the direction of the field . . . a ban on cloning could lead the best researchers . . . to avoid the field entirely.*

When the genotype donor has been selected because of his or her accomplishments, cloning would also seem to place the child in a no-win situation. The child's successes will be regarded as genetically inevitable while failures are likely to be attributed to an unwillingness to make the efforts needed to materialize his or her genetic promise. Finally, when intrafamilial cloning is involved (the cloning of a child who is the genetic replica of a parent), some fear that all these concerns may be compounded by problems of excessive intimacy and interdependency between parents and child.

The faulty premise of genetic determinism

What are we to say about these scenarios of psychic damage? First, if true, they represent a level of harm to the child that warrants concern. The fact that these harms will not be immediately observable and that significant injury may not be evident until long after many cloned children are born makes it reasonable to ask whether cloning should be allowed in the first place. How likely, however, are these harms to occur? A major problem here, as many have noted, is that the reasoning rests on the fallacious premise that our genes strictly determine us: that genotype is phenotype. Although genes do influence many features of our physical, intellectual, and temperamental make-up, they are only one factor in the complex web of events that shape our life. Interactions with the environment from the moment of conception onward profoundly influence the expression of genes. In the words of geneticist Richard Lewontin:

> The fallacy of genetic determinism is to suppose that the genes "make" the organism. It is a basic principle of developmental biology that organisms undergo a continuous development from conception to death, a development that is a unique consequence of the interaction of the genes in their cells, the temporal sequence of environments through which the organisms pass, and random cellular processes. . . . As a result, even the fingerprints of identical twins are not identical. Their temperaments, mental processes, abilities, life choices, disease histories, and deaths certainly differ, despite the determined efforts of many parents to enforce as great a similarity as possible.

What does the faulty premise of genetic determinism mean for these arguments about speculative psychological harms? First of all, it suggests that in cases where parents are well informed of their limited ability to use cloning to determine a child's talents or disposition, many of the feared pressures and expectations will not exist. Parents may choose to use cloning to have a child more genetically related to one of them than would be true with other reproductive alternatives, but they will not bring to this the unreasonable expectation that the child will necessarily be very much like the genotype donor. This does not mean that parents may not harbor some wish that Mary will share her mother's passion (or ability) for ballet. Even the parents of sexually produced children, however, have such expectations and frequently do all they can to impose their wishes on children. . . .

As a general rule, in seeking to prevent injury it is always ethically required to select the most efficacious and least restrictive means possible. Because cloning can benefit people, the aim is to permit people to use it while eliminating those aspects of it that lead directly to harm. This suggests that the proper mode of intervention is not to ban cloning but to reduce the ignorance and misinformation that can make it harmful. We can do this by requiring psychological workups and counseling for parents as a condition of their participation in cloning programs. Critics of cloning, in their haste to construct scenarios of possible harm, have often failed to consider the range of alternatives for minimizing damage. . . .

Criticisms of the National Bioethics Advisory Commission report

I want to conclude this ethical review of the cloning controversy by offering a brief critique of the National Bioethics Advisory Commission (NBAC) report. . . .

The NBAC called for a uniform federal ban on any attempt to clone a human being. The commission would permit human research as long as it was not intended to lead to the birth of a cloned child, and it also recommended a 3 to 5 year "sunset provision" in any legislation to allow reconsideration of the issue in the future. These recommendations seem moderate, but they are actually quite radical. A federal ban, however circumscribed, shifts the emphasis from regulated support to outright prohibition.

Instead of inviting the best scientists to assume responsibility for the direction of the field in concert with the existing human subjects review process, a ban on cloning could lead the best researchers and institutions to avoid the field entirely. This would leave cloning to irresponsible scientists at the margins of the profession. The argument that good preliminary research could still take place in this country as long as it did not aim at the birth of a child is undercut by the existing legal prohibitions of federal funding for embryo research. Deprived of federal support, researchers committed to perfecting human cloning may well find themselves attracted to more permissive jurisdictions overseas or may seek employment in offshore commercial enterprises offering cloning for a price. None of these outcomes enhances the possibility of good ethical oversight of this research.

The idea that Congress might act in the future to reconsider or lift a cloning ban is also naive. New reproductive technologies are caught up in our deep divisions over the abortion question and our polarized moral views on the status of the early embryo. In these debates, the legislative process is particularly vulnerable to pressure from militant minority groups. For nearly 20 years, federal funding for embryo research has been blocked by a coalition of "pro-life" groups. Similarly, once a federal law against human cloning is enacted, a small number of dedicated opponents can work to keep it in place. By urging a ban, the NBAC opened the door to this possibility.

Embryonic research is needed to assess risks

My final criticism has to do with the NBAC's decision not to make any recommendations about the issue of human embryo research as it relates to cloning. There were some very good reasons why the NBAC chose to bypass this issue. For one thing, its members rightly concluded that the most worrisome risks at this time have to do with the damage that cloning might do to any children born through this still undeveloped procedure. This meant that there was no reason to prohibit private cloning research using embryos as long as no effort was made to transfer these embryos to a womb. By not supporting a private sector ban on cloning research when no transfer was involved, the NBAC also refused to add its voice to those who would take advantage of the cloning controversy to further restrict embryo research in this country.

The real question, however, is why the NBAC failed to issue a more urgent appeal for federally funded research on cloning when no transfer [to the womb] was intended. . . .

In answering this question, we must recall that the principal rationale behind the NBAC's call for a ban on human cloning were the unknown risks of this procedure for the child. If this ban were to be reconsidered in five years' time, as the NBAC recommended, we would thus need a body of experimental data offering a more precise idea of the risks full human cloning would entail. But how were we to learn about these risks? Research using human embryos not intended for transfer would be crucial, yet federal support for such research was prohibited. This means that the burden of providing the information needed for a critical review of the federal ban would fall on private research facilities that had few resources for such studies and that were largely exempt from human subjects regulations.

NBAC fails to resolve larger cloning issues

If the NBAC's members really believed that the most pressing questions around cloning concerned safety to the child, they would seem to have had an obligation to make clear the urgent need for federally funded research in this area. That they did not do so tells me that they never really seriously considered the matter of immediate risks or how they might be assessed and reduced. Rather, the emphasis on these risks was a convenient way for the NBAC to ratify and continue the moratorium instituted by the President without having to resolve all the larger questions about cloning that had been raised.

The NBAC's approach here may be reasonable. I do not want to revisit the difficult choices the commission had to make to sustain its value and credibility. Nevertheless, the approach they took provides a vivid illustration of some of the dynamics whose presence in our ethical debates I have tried to signal. One is the sense of panic and the pressure toward prohibition that has accompanied this technology from the start. Our discussions about cloning have too often been an impulse toward prohibition in search of a rationale. Closely related to this is the tendency to posit risks without critical scrutiny of their likelihood or gravity. Highly speculative scenarios have been constructed with little examination of their logic, or, as in the case of the NBAC report, concrete risks have been alleged with no recommendations for how they might be measured or reduced. Finally, too little attention has been given to the other side of the issue: the reasons why cloning or cloning research might be advisable or the harms of prohibitions and research obstructions. Cloning critics have sometimes lived in a cost-free world where innovative research might be stopped by fiat with little price in terms of lost knowledge, undeveloped therapies, or damage to the research enterprise.

The immediate controversy around cloning has not been one of our better moments in the formation of public science policy. I have tried to signal some of the ways contributors to this debate have erred or exaggerated in their approach to the issues, and I have tried to highlight modes of reasoning that, although understandable, skew our discussions and block reasoned deliberation. By taking stock of the excesses in these debates, we can improve our response to cloning and other biomedical innovations in the future.

8

Cloning Humans Is Unethical

President's Council on Bioethics

The President's Council on Bioethics was created by President George W. Bush on November 28, 2001, to examine the moral significance of developments in biomedical and behavioral science and technology and explore specific ethical and policy questions. Its members are seventeen leading scientists, doctors, ethicists, social scientists, lawyers, and theologians. The council is chaired by Leon Kass, a prominent bioethicist from the University of Chicago.

Human reproductive cloning is an issue with many wide-reaching ramifications. First, basic human rights are at stake. It is impossible to ask an unconceived human clone if it wants to undergo the high medical risks being born a clone entails. Cloned children may also suffer from a reduced sense of individuality and freedom. Furthermore, cloning could be done for the unethical purpose of trying to create "superior" humans with traits arbitrarily valued by a particular culture. The process could likewise result in the dehumanization and commercialization of clones and their progenitors. Finally, the consequences of altering the human gene pool through cloning are unknown. Cloning poses many threats to society, which must carefully consider whether it wants to allow it.

The arguments put forward in defense of "reproductive" cloning tend to strike the ear at first as familiar and congenial because they generally address themselves to subjects we are quite used to dealing with in our political and public life: to

President's Council on Bioethics, "Staff Working Paper 3b: Arguments Against 'Reproductive Cloning,'" www.bioethics.gov, January 2002.

individual rights, to the satisfaction of personal desires, to the exercise of human will. Modern liberal democratic politics is especially good at thinking about these human goods and at providing for them. Arguments against permitting human cloning have a far less familiar ring to them, because while they do draw on some of the most prominent and important liberal premises (for instance by pointing to serious concerns about safety and consent, among others) they also draw upon a rather different set of human goods, to which our politics does not often address itself explicitly: human dignity and worth; human bonds, both natural and social; the freedom that can come only from certain sorts of limits on the human will; the meaning and the power of our procreative nature and its relation to our mortality. These are, in many ways, the highest human things, but they are not always, and should not be always, political things; and so our politics does not often think of them. We human individuals, however, do think about them. They speak to us often more clearly and directly than do the theories of individual rights and the promise of comfort and even of health. For the most part, we are quite well able to keep these two realms—one higher but less political, the other lower but more immediate and practical—separate. But when the two fall into conflict, we are challenged to prioritize among them.

We must take an active role

The prospect of twenty-first century biotechnology forces us to think of this, because it threatens to bring the two realms into conflict. It does so precisely because the powers it makes possible are to be used on the bodies and minds of human beings, and in ways that go beyond the traditional medical goal of healing the sick. In their quest for comfort and health, advocates of human cloning seek to give new form to human procreation—and we must think of what that might do to all the human goods that are connected in countless subtle ways to human procreation. In their desire to empower human will, they seek to break the mold of natural human limitation—and we must think of where a new standard of human behavior and dignity might come from. In their quest for the empowerment of individuals, they raise questions that human societies can answer only together—and we must face these questions and consider them carefully before we decide how we ought to proceed.

All the human goods in question—individual rights, the

quest for health and longer life, the desire for a biologically related child, the desire for freedom, human dignity, human humility and wonder, and the procreative character of human
life—are of great importance to us; but as biology and medicine
seek out new powers, some of these goods may come into conflict with others. It will be up to us, as individuals and particularly as political communities, to address these conflicts, and in
doing so we must take an active role and not simply let things
fall where they may. The stakes are too high for passivity. The
promise is too great. The risks are too serious. And we must deliberate carefully to reach the wisest judgment and to determine the best course of action. In making this judgment, we
must understand and we must articulate as clearly as possible
both sets of human goods: not only the one we are very good
at talking about, but also the other, which we rarely speak of,
but which we find impossible to ignore. . . .

Safety and health issues in human cloning

Risks to the cloned child must be taken especially seriously, not
least because—unlike the risks to the egg donor and surrogate
mother—they cannot be accepted knowingly and freely by the
person who will bear them. The risks to the cloned child have
at this point led nearly everyone involved in the debate to consider cloning thoroughly unsafe. In animal experiments to
date, only approximately 5 percent of attempts to clone have
resulted in live births, and a substantial portion of those live-
born clones have suffered complications that proved fatal fairly
quickly. Longer term consequences are of course not known,
since the oldest successfully cloned mammal is only approximately five years of age.[1] Some medium-term consequences, including premature aging, immune system failures, and sudden
unexplained deaths, have already become apparent in some
cloned mammals.

Furthermore, there are concerns that a cell from an individual who has lived for some years may have accumulated genetic mutations which—if used in the cloning of a new human
life—may predispose the new individual to certain sorts of cancer and other diseases.

Along with these threats to the health and well being of the

1. Dolly, the world's first cloned mammal, was euthanized in February 2003 at
age six, due to premature aging.

cloned child, there appear to exist some risks to the health of the egg donor (particularly risks to her future reproductive health caused by the hormonal treatments required for egg donation) and risks to the health of the surrogate mother (for instance, animal experiments suggest a higher than average likelihood of overweight offspring, which can adversely affect the health of the birth-mother). . . .

The right to consent

Beyond physical safety, the prospect of "reproductive" cloning also raises concerns about a potential violation of the rights of individuals, particularly through a denial of the right to consent to the use of one's body in experimentation or medical procedures.

Consent from the human clone itself is of course impossible to obtain. It may be argued, on the one hand, that no one consents to his own birth, so concerns about consent are misplaced when applied to the unborn. But the issue is not so simple. For reasons having much to do with the safety concerns raised above and the social and psychological concerns to be addressed below, an attempt to clone a human being would expose the cloned individual-to-be to great risks of harm, in addition to, and different from, those accompanying other sorts of reproduction. Given the risks, and the fact that consent cannot be obtained, the ethical choice may be to avoid the experiment.

> *Once the natural goal of health has been blurred out of existence, medicine will come to serve only ends designed by human will, and thus may have no limits.*

Against this point it might be said that the alternative to cloning is for the cloned individual not to exist at all, and that no one would prefer non-existence to the chance at life. Such an argument, however, could easily come to be used as an excuse for absolutely any use and abuse of embryonic or newborn life. Giving life to an individual does not grant one the right to harm that individual. It is true that the scientist cannot ask an unconceived child for permission, but this puts a burden on the scientist, not on the child. All that the scientist can know is that he or she is putting a newly created life at enormous risk; and given that knowledge, the ethics of human experimentation suggest that the best option is to avoid the procedure altogether. . . .

Reengineering humans

Human "reproductive" cloning could also come to be used for eugenic purposes: that is, in an attempt to alter (with the aim of improving) the genetic constitution of future generations. Indeed, that is the stated purpose of some proponents of "reproductive" cloning, and has been at the heart of much support for the concept of "reproductive" cloning for decades. Proponents of eugenics were once far more open regarding their intentions and their hopes to escape the uncertain lottery of sex and reach an era of controlled and humanly directed reproduction, which would allow future generations to suffer fewer genetic defects and to enjoy more advantageous genotypes. In the present debate, the case for eugenics is not made quite so openly, but it nonetheless remains an important driving motivation for some proponents of human cloning, and a potential use of "reproductive" cloning.

Cloning can serve the ends of eugenics either by avoiding the genetic defects that may arise when human reproduction is left to natural chance; or by preserving and perpetuating outstanding genetic traits. In the future, if techniques for precise genetic engineering become available, cloning could be useful for perpetuating the enhanced traits created by such techniques, and for keeping the "superior" man-made genotype free of the flaws that sexual reproduction might otherwise introduce.

The darkest side of eugenics is of course familiar to any student of the twentieth century. Its central place in Nazi ideology, and its brutal and inhuman application by the Third Reich, have put that science largely out of favor. No argument in today's cloning debate bears any resemblance to those of Hitler's doctors. But by the same token, it is not primarily the Nazi analogy that should lead us to reject eugenics.

It is a less dark side of eugenic science that threatens to confront us. This side is well-intentioned but could prove at least as dangerous to our humanity. The eugenic goal of "better" and "healthy" children combined with modern genetic techniques threatens to blur and ultimately eliminate the line between therapy and enhancement. Medicine is guided by the natural standard of health. It is by this standard that we judge who is in need of medical treatment, and what sort of treatment might be most appropriate. The doctor's purpose is to restore a sick patient to health. Indeed, we even practice a kind of "negative" eugenics guided by this standard: as when parents choose to abort a fetus who has been diagnosed with a serious genetic disease. This "negative eugenics" may be morally problematic in itself, but it is at least a practice that is informed by a standard of health.

Good intentions may go astray

The "positive" eugenics that could receive a great boost from human "reproductive" cloning does not seek to restore human beings to natural health when they are ill. Instead, it seeks to alter humanity, based upon a standard of man's (or some men's) own making. Once the natural goal of health has been blurred out of existence, medicine will come to serve only ends designed by human will, and thus may have no limits, may feel no constraints, and may respect no barriers. Reproduction itself might come to serve one or another purely man-made end, and future generations may come to be products of our artful and rational design more than extensions of our humanity. All of this may well be guided by what plainly seem like good intentions: to improve the next generation, to enhance the quality of life of our descendants, to let our children do more than we ourselves could do. But in the process, we stand to lose the very means by which to judge the goodness or the wisdom of the particular aims proposed by a positive eugenics. We stand to lose the sense of what is and is not human; a set of limits on our hubris; a standard against which to judge the legitimacy of certain human actions. All of these, along with the specific traits and characteristics done away with in the process of eugenic enhancement, could be lost. "Reproductive" cloning may well contribute to these losses. . . .

In addition, eugenics may also open the road to a new inequality, by which only those who can afford it can procure advantages for themselves and their descendants into future generations. A situation in which only the rich can grant their children high IQs, broad shoulders and long lives would prove unbearable to a liberal democracy, and might either lead to serious social tension or more likely to a government entitlement to genetic enhancement and manipulation—managed by the state.

By serving the ends of eugenics, "reproductive" cloning may open the door to all of these various difficulties.

Human intervention creates unforeseen consequences

Cloning also raises a number of concerns about humanity's relation with the natural world. The precautionary principle, which informs the ideals of the environmental movement, may have something to say to us about cloning. It urges us to beware of the unintended consequences of applications of human power and will—particularly over nature. Natural systems of great complexity do not respond well to blunt human intervention, and one can hardly think of a more complex system than that responsible for human reproduction. This principle suggests that geneticists should not pretend to understand the consequences of their profound alterations of human nature, and lacking such understanding they should not take actions so drastic as the cloning of a human child.

The ethic of environmentalism also preaches a respect for nature as we find it, and argues that the complex structure of the natural world has much to teach us. Such an ethic therefore disapproves of efforts aimed at simply overcoming nature as we find it, and imposing a man-made process over a slowly evolved natural process. It opposes the hubristic overconfidence inherent in the cloning project, and fears that such a project may erase the boundary between the natural and the technological.

In addition, cloning, in the unlikely event it should become commonplace, may diminish the diversity of the human gene-pool. Sexual reproduction introduces unique combinations of genes into the human gene-pool, while eugenic cloning aimed at reproducing particular genotypes will tend to diminish that diversity, and with it the "strength" of the species. Eugenic enhancement may thus "weaken" future generations.

Human clones would be manufactured products

"Reproductive" cloning could also represent an enormous step in the direction of transforming human procreation into human manufacture. . . .

Human "reproductive" cloning, and the forms of human manufacture it might make possible, would begin with a very specific end-product in mind, and would be tailored to produce that product. Scientists or parents would set out to produce specific individuals for particular reasons, and the individuals might well come to be subjected to those reasons. The procreative process could come to be seen as a means of meeting some very specific ends, and the resulting children would be products of a designed manufacturing process: means to the satisfaction of a particular desire, or to some other end. They would be means, not ends in themselves.

> *'Reproductive' cloning could . . . represent an enormous step in the direction of transforming human procreation into human manufacture.*

Things made by man stand subservient to the man who made them. Manufactured goods are always understood to have been made to serve a purpose, not to exist independently and freely. Scientists who clone (or even merely breed) animals make no secret of the instrumental purposes behind their actions—they act with specific instrumental ends in mind, and the resulting animals are means to that preexisting end. Human cloning threatens to introduce the same approach and the same attitudes into human procreation.

The transformation of human procreation into human manufacture could thus result in a radical dehumanization of the resulting children, as well as of those who set out to clone, and by its effect on societal attitudes also a dehumanization of everyone else. When we become able to look upon some human beings as manufactured goods, no matter how perfect, we may become less able to look upon any human beings as fully independent persons, endowed with liberty and deserving of respect and dignity. . . .

The commercialism of human reproduction

"Reproductive" cloning presents us with the potential for a market in clones of particular outstanding individuals (as in some sense already occurs with existing techniques when potential parents seek egg or sperm donors with high IQs or deep blue eyes); or more generally for the further encroachment of market principles and profit motives into the realm of human procreation. Present techniques already point the way toward a world of celebrity cell auctions and rent-a-womb agencies, and the widespread use of human "reproductive" cloning might very well get us there.

The concerns expressed here—and, indeed, throughout this critique of cloning—do not depend on cloning becoming a very widespread practice. On the contrary, even small scale markets, say, in celebrity cloning, could affect far more than just the lives of those individuals who are involved in particular transactions within them. The acceptance of such markets by society would affect the way everyone thinks about the issues at stake. The adoption of market terms and ideas in the arena of human moral choices could easily blind us to genuine moral issues. The reconceptualization of society as a system of rent-seeking, of human life as a scarce good in demand, and of moral wrongs as mere costs, could make us far less capable of reasoning thoughtfully about our status and responsibilities as human beings. . . .

Our genetic uniqueness

Our genetic uniqueness, manifested externally in our looks and our fingerprints and internally in our immune systems, is one source of our sense of freedom and independence. It symbolizes our autonomy and it endows us with a sense of possibility. Each of us knows that no one has ever had our unique combination of natural characteristics before. We know that no one knows all the potentialities contained within that combination. A cloned child, however, will live out a life shaped by a genotype that has already lived. However much or little this may actually mean in terms of hard scientific fact, it could mean a great deal to that individual's experience of life. He or she may be constantly held up to the model of the source of his or her cloned genotype, or may (consciously and unconsciously) hold himself or herself up to that model. He or she would be denied the opportunity to live a life that in all respects has never been lived before, and (perhaps more importantly) might know things about his or her own genetic destiny that may constrain his or her range of options and sense of freedom.

It may be reasonably argued that genetic individuality as such is not an essential human good, since identical twins share a common genotype and seem not to be harmed by it. But this argument misses entirely the context and environment into which a human clone would be born. Identical twins are born together, before either one has developed and shown what his or her potential—natural or otherwise—may be. They are each largely free of the burden of measuring up to or even just knowing the genetic traits of the other, since neither twin is yet known to the world. But a clone is the twin of a person who is already (or was) living. Moreover, he or she was cloned from that person's DNA for a reason, and must therefore in one way or another deal with his or her connection to that person and that reason. This would constrain the clone's individuality or sense of self in ways that differ in kind from the experience of identical twins. The key, again, is the cloned individual's life as that individual experiences it, and not just the scientific question of the extent to which genetic identity actually shapes us.

> *It could prove very difficult for the cloned individual to step outside the shadow of his progenitor, and to live a truly new, unique, and free and independent life.*

In these ways, even though genotype is certainly not destiny, the cloned individual and the society around him may come to place too much importance on the genotype, because as something known it is something which can be analyzed. By leading this individual to be judged in relation to his genetically virtually identical twin source in a way that others are not judged, his status as a clone could turn that origin into a kind of destiny, and might sharply constrain his freedom and sense of identity. It could prove very difficult for the cloned individual to step outside the shadow of his progenitor, and to live a truly new, unique, and free and independent life.

A harmed sense of individuality and freedom

The cloned individual's sense of independence could also suffer because of his status as a being made to order by another. Children conceived by sexual reproduction (even with the aid of IVF [in vitro fertilization]) know that they, like all human beings before them, entered the world as something of a surprise.

No parent knows exactly what to expect, and so every good parent is willing to accept what comes and to welcome the children as they are. . . .

But the cloned child does not (or at the very least may think he does not) share such a relationship with his parents. The cloned child will have been created by the deliberate design of parents or scientists, and thus his relation to others will be fundamentally different from that of naturally conceived individuals. A begotten child stands in the same relation to the world as his parents; a created child—any kind of manufactured or designed child—does not. He stands beneath his parents and others in a way that children generally do not: as a human artifact designed and constructed. This fact of his origins almost cannot help but harm the cloned person's sense of individuality and freedom.

At the same time that our procreative origins endow us with individuality and freedom, our natural connection to our family of origin also binds us to the human world in ways that matter deeply. Personal and social identity and social links of responsibility are connected in countless ways to ties of biological kinship. The psychic identity of the cloned individual, already troubled by a diminished sense of individuality as mentioned above, could be much further troubled by the utter confusion of kinship relations that would result from the circumstances of its origins.

Connection to family

Just as the cloned individual's sense of individuality may be confused by his origin, his connection to others, and particularly to their own family, may become muddled as well. Moreover, this effect could be mirrored and amplified in the effect that cloning might have on the institution of the family, and the way in which individuals and communities come to think of procreation.

The clone's place in the scheme of human relations will be uncertain and confused. The usual clear designations of father and mother, sister and brother, would be confounded. The clone would have only one genetic parent, his or her connection to grandparents would span both one and two generations at once, and every other family relation would be similarly confused. Even if the child was cloned from someone who is not a member of the family in which the child is raised, the fact would remain (and may be known to the child) that he or she has been created in the nearly precise genetic image of another, for some particular reason with some particular design in mind. This is far from the way children generally (and naturally) relate to their family of origin, and the differences may tend to run against the grain of the social institutions that surround the family. . . .

The confusion created by the complicated relationship of cloner to cloned may mean that no clear lines of parent-child, sibling-sibling, or other familial kin relations will develop. These vital links could be subject to serious confusion and uncertainty, and so the model of the natural family would be very difficult if not impossible to emulate. By breaking through the natural boundaries between generations, cloning threatens to undo the social links between them. A clone of oneself is a brother and a son, or a sister and a daughter. Should you relate to him or her as parent or as sibling? Neither relationship could take form very well under the strains of the peculiarly muddled natural relation established by cloning.

The point may be made thus: Existing family relationships are either drawn from or based upon the relationships that naturally arise from the process of human procreation. Cloning not only does not point naturally to these relations, it actively opposes them by undermining their foundations, especially the relationships between generations. The cloned child's psychic health and sense of identity may well be placed in jeopardy.

And the family, as an institution, may be harmed as well. The family, of course, is at once a social and a natural institution, and the two elements reinforce each other in countless subtle ways. Breaking some of the links between them could leave the institution of the family without a firm grounding in nature and without strong social support. . . .

Parental expectations

Rather than accept whatever child they turn out to have given rise to, parents [of a cloned child] determine in advance what sort of child they will accept. The resulting child is much more the product of these expectations than a child conceived in the natural way would be. Such a cloned child is likely to be regarded more like a possession of its parents, or even an instrument of their will, than a normally conceived child would be. The parents begin their child's life with an overbearing act that must be said to border on despotism. They begin the new child's life by restricting the new child's independence and individuality. The family, in this way, loses something of its character as a nursery of a novel and independent new human generation, and gains something of the character of an instrument of the present generation. This does not mean that the parents are ill-intentioned, but it could very well mean that their children are less free to flourish. The character of families thus changes in ways we may not like.

> **❝***A clone of oneself is a brother and a son, or a sister and a daughter. Should you relate to him or her as parent or as sibling?* **❞**

Other, more immediately concrete, troubles may confront family life as well. The parents of a cloned child may find themselves unable to treat a child who is the clone of someone they have known (let alone of themselves) in the way that parents may presently treat a child generated sexually. Such a cloned child would be born with an unnatural and perhaps unhealthy relation to someone (past or present) in the world, and this could make healthy family life more difficult.

In addition, the presence of human clones may over time tend to undermine society's sense of what a family relationship means and how it relates to nature, sex and reproduction. The distance between the procreative nature of humanity and the social status of the family could grow, and both may become less thoroughly grounded in one another. That grounding, as has been discussed, is vital for both, and its diminution could bring with it profound problems. Family relations, and social relations in general, are founded at the deepest level on mankind's procreative nature, and on our character as begotten and begetting creatures. Undoing that nature and that character may tend to undo the roots and the foundations of family structure and family life. Much about the way we live as human beings has to do with our procreative nature: begetting and belonging condition the way we think of our place in the world, our place among human beings, our place in time, our mortality. Society is structured around all of these things.

Human institutions, and particularly those (like the family) that transcend specific times and places, are storehouses of human wisdom. They possess in their very structure more intelligence and experience than do the thoughts and ideas of any particular generation. Undoing these institutions, as "reproductive" cloning may begin to do, would very likely have far greater repercussions than we can fully contemplate.

Impact on society

These repercussions, moreover, would not be limited to the lives of individuals and families directly affected by cloning. Indeed, the impact of human "reproductive" cloning on society at large may be the least appreciated, but among the most important, factors to consider in contemplating a public policy on human cloning.

> *A society that clones human beings is a society that thinks about human beings differently than a society that refuses to do so.*

Cloning is a human activity, which affects not only those who are cloned or who are clones, but also the entire society that allows or that supports (and therefore that engages in) such activity—as would be the case with a society that allows some of its members to practice slavery, to take a most extreme example. The question before us is whether "reproductive" cloning is an activity that we, as a society, should engage in. In addressing this question, we must reach well beyond the rights of individuals, and the difficulties or benefits that cloned children or their families might encounter. The question we must face has to do with what we, as a society, will permit ourselves to do. When we say that "reproductive" cloning may erode our respect for the dignity of human beings, we must say that we, as a society that engages in cloning, would be responsible for that erosion. When we argue that vital social institutions could be harmed, we must acknowledge that it is we, as a society that clones, that would be harming them. We should not ask if "reproductive" cloning is something that some people somewhere should be permitted to do. We must ask if cloning is something that all of us together should want to do or should allow ourselves to do. Insofar as we permit cloning in our society, we are the cloners and the cloned, just as we are the society affected by the process. Only when we see that do we understand our responsibility in crafting a public policy regarding human "reproductive" cloning.

Since we are the ones acting to clone, we must further realize that our actions will affect us not only in what they directly do to us, but also in the way they shape our thinking. A society that clones human beings is a society that thinks about human beings differently than a society that refuses to do so. We must therefore also ask ourselves how we as a society prefer to think of human beings. . . .

Doing nothing about such a subject is not an option. If we as a society refrain from considering the question entirely, we would—implicitly—be saying yes to cloning, with all that such a statement would entail. We face the choice only of engaging in cloning or forbidding it, and the option we select will say a lot about us. Given the issues involved, there is no neutral ground for the polity to hold in this particular debate.

Society exists beyond individuals, beyond generations. And among the highest tasks of any society is the management of its relation to the future, and the transmission of its institutions and its ideals to the next generation. As we have seen, it is here, at this vital junction of the generations, that cloning threatens to wreak havoc, and this junction is insufficiently protected by the market and by private interests. It is here that cloning poses a special challenge to society, and it is here that politics becomes important in meeting that challenge.

9

Embryonic Stem Cell Research Is Ethical

Michael D. West

Michael D. West is president, chairman, and CEO of Advanced Cell Technology, Inc., a biotechnology company developing potential medical applications of nuclear transfer (cloning) and embryonic stem cell technologies. He is the author of The Immortal Cell, *and coeditor of* Principles of Cloning. *West has written extensively for scientific journals and holds dozens of patents relating to genomics. He founded the Geron Corporation in Menlo Park, California, in 1990. He served as director and vice president until 1998, managing programs for human embryonic stem cell research. He is also the founder and former chairman of Origen Therapeutics, Inc., a privately held biotechnology company in Burlingame, California.*

One must understand the facts about human reproduction and embryonic stem (ES) cells to make informed ethical decisions about the use of ES cells in medical applications. Scientific evidence establishes decisively that individual human life does not begin until fourteen days after fertilization. Researchers use the human embryonic stem cells that develop before human life begins. The stem cell technologies they are developing could solve many medical dilemmas, including the problem of tissue compatibility. Therapeutic cloning would allow scientists to grow new tissue identical to that of the patient, preventing transplant rejection and resulting in fewer complications. The lifesaving potential of stem cell technology is enormous. It is society's moral duty to use the gifts of stem cell research to help people overcome disease.

Michael D. West, testimony before the U.S. Senate Appropriations Committee, Subcommittee on Labor, Health and Human Services, and Education, Washington, DC, July 18, 2001.

Editor's Note: This selection is Michael D. West's testimony before the U.S. Senate Appropriations Committee, Labor, Health and Human Services, and Education Subcommittee on July 18, 2001, regarding embryonic stem cell and nuclear transfer technologies.

I am pleased to testify today in regard to the new opportunities and challenges associated with human embryonic stem (ES) cell and nuclear transfer (NT) [cloning] technologies. I will begin by describing the bright promise of these twin and interrelated technologies and then attempt to correct some misunderstandings relating to their application in medicine.

It may be useful to point out that I think of myself as pro-life in that I have an enormous respect for the value of the individual human life. Indeed, in my years following college I joined others in the protest of abortion clinics. My goal was not to send a message to women that they did not have the right to choose. My intent was simply to urge them to reconsider the destruction of a developing human being. Despite my strong convictions about the value of the individual human life, in 1995 I organized the collaboration between [biopharmaceutical] Geron Corporation and the laboratories of Drs. James Thomson and John Gearhart [both holders of U.S.-approved patents for human embryonic stem cell lines] to isolate embryonic stem cells and human embryonic germ cells from human embryos and fetuses respectively. My reasons were simple. These technologies are entirely designed to be used in medicine to alleviate human suffering and to save human life. They are, in fact, pro-life. The opponents that argue they destroy human lives are simply and tragically mistaken. Let me explain why this is the case.

When human life begins

We are composed of trillions of individual living cells, glued together like the bricks of a building to construct the organs and tissues of our body. The cells in our bodies are called "somatic cells" to distinguish them from the "germ line", that is, the reproductive cells that connect the generations. We now know that life evolved from such single-celled organisms that dominated all life some one billion years ago.

Therefore, in answer to the question of when life begins, we must make a crucial distinction. Biological life, that is to say, "cellular life" has no recent beginnings. Our cells are, in fact, the descendents of cells that trace their beginnings to the origin of life on earth. However, when we speak of an individual human life, we are speaking of the communal life of a multicellular organism springing from the reproductive lineage of cells. The individual human life is a body composed of cells committed to somatic cell lineages. All somatic cells are related in that they originate from an original cell formed from the union of a sperm and egg cell.

The fertilization of the egg cell by a sperm leads to a single cell called the "zygote". From this first cell, multiple rounds of cell division over the first week result in a microscopic ball of cells with very unusual properties. This early embryo, called the "preimplantation embryo", has not implanted in the uterus to begin a pregnancy. It is estimated that approximately 40% of preimplantation embryos formed following normal human sexual reproduction fail to attach to the uterus and are naturally destroyed as a result.

> *Approximately 40% of preimplantation embryos formed . . . fail to attach to the uterus and are naturally destroyed as a result.*

At the blastocyst stage of the preimplantation embryo, no body cells of any type have formed, and even more significantly, there is strong evidence that not even the earliest of events in the chain of events in somatic differentiation[1] have been initiated. A simple way of demonstrating this is by observing subsequent events.

Should the embryo implant in the uterus, the embryo, at approximately 14 days post fertilization will form what is called the primitive streak, this is the first definition that these "seed" cells will form an individual human being as opposed to the forming of two primitive streaks leading to identical twins. Rarely two primitive streaks form that are not completely separated leading to conjoined or Siamese twins. In addition, rarely, two separately fertilized egg cells fuse together to form a single embryo with two different cell types. This natural event

1. in which the cells begin to form the various parts of the body

leads to a tetragammetic chimera, that is a single human individual with some of the cells in their body being male from the original male embryo, and some cells being female from the original female embryo. These and other simple lessons in embryology teach us that despite the dogmatic assertions of some theologians, the evidence is decisive in support of the position that an individual human life, as opposed to merely cellular life, begins with the primitive streak, (i.e. after 14 days of development). Those who argue that the preimplantation embryo is a person are left with the logical absurdity of ascribing to the blastocyst personhood when we know, scientifically speaking, that no individual exists (i.e. the blastocyst may still form identical twins).

The lifesaving potential of human ES cells

Human ES cells are nothing other than ICM [inner cell mass] cells grown in the laboratory dish. Because these are pure stem cells uncommitted to any body cell lineage, they may greatly improve the availability of diverse cell types urgently needed in medicine. Human ES cells are unique in that they stand near the base of the developmental tree. These cells are frequently designated "totipotent" stem cells, meaning that they are potentially capable of forming any cell or tissue type needed in medicine. These differ from adult stem cells that are "pluripotent" that is, capable of forming several, but only a limited number, of cell types. An example of pluripotent adult stem cells are the bone marrow stem cells now widely used in the treatment of cancer and other life-threatening diseases.

> *The belief that an individual human being begins with the fertilization of the egg cell by the sperm cell is without basis in scientific fact.*

Some have voiced objection to the use of human ES cells in medicine owing to the source of the cells. Whereas the use of these new technologies has already been carefully debated and approved in the United Kingdom, the United States lags disgracefully behind. I would like to think it is our goodness and our kindness as a people that generates our country's anxieties over these new technologies. Indeed, early in my life I might have argued that since we don't know when a human life begins, it is best not to tamper with the early embryo. That is to say, it is better to be safe than sorry. I believe many U.S. citizens share this initial reaction. But, with time the facts of human embryology and cell biology will be more widely understood. As the Apostle Paul said: "When I was a child, I spake as a child, I understood as a child, I thought as a child: but when I became a man, I put away childish things." (I Cor 13:11) In the same way it is absolutely a matter of life and death that policy makers in the United States carefully study the facts of human embryology and stem cells. A child's understanding of human reproduction simply will not suffice and such ignorance could lead to disastrous consequences.

With appropriate funding of research, we may soon learn to direct these cells to become vehicles of lifesaving potential. We may, for instance, become able to produce neurons for the treatment of Parkinson's disease and spinal cord injury, heart muscle cells for heart failure, cartilage for arthritis and many others as well. This research has great potential to help solve the first problem of tissue availability, but the technologies to direct these cells to become various cell types in adequate quantities remains to be elucidated. Because literally hundreds of cell types are needed, thousands of academic research projects need to be funded, far exceeding the resources of the biotechnology industry.

As promising as ES cell technology may seem, it does not solve the remaining problem of histocompatibility [tissue compatibility to allow grafting]. Human ES cells obtained from embryos derived during in vitro fertilization procedures, or from fetal sources, are essentially cells from another individual. . . .

Therapeutic cloning solves the problem of cell compatibility

An extremely promising solution to this remaining problem of histocompatibility would be to create human ES cells genetically identical to the patient. While no ES cells are known to exist in a developed human being and are therefore not available as a source for therapy, such cells could possibly be obtained through the procedure of somatic cell nuclear transfer (NT), otherwise known as cloning technology. In this procedure, body cells from a patient would be fused with an egg cell that has had its nuclear DNA removed. This would theoretically allow the production of a blastocyst-staged embryo genetically identical to the patient that could, in turn, lead to the production of ES cells identical to the patient. In addition, published data suggests that the procedure of NT can "rejuvenate" an aged cell restoring the proliferative capacity inherent in cells at the beginning of life. This could lead to cellular therapies with an unprecedented opportunity to improve the quality of life for an aging population.

The use of somatic cell nuclear transfer for the purposes of dedifferentiating a patient's cells and obtain autologous undifferentiated stem cells has been designated "Therapeutic Cloning" or alternatively, "Cell Replacement by Nuclear Transfer". This terminology is used to differentiate this clinical indication from the use of NT for the cloning of a child that in turn is designated "Reproductive Cloning". In the United Kingdom, the use of NT for therapeutic cloning has been carefully studied by their Embryology Authority and formally approved by the Parliament.

Ethical considerations

Ethical debates often center over two separate lines of reasoning. Deontological debates are, by nature, focused on our duty to God or our fellow human being. Teleological arguments focus on the question of whether the ends justify the means. Most scholars agree that human ES cell technology and therapeutic cloning offer great pragmatic merit, that is, the teleological arguments in favor of ES and NT technologies are quite strong. The lack of agreement, instead, centers on the deontological arguments relating to the rights of the blastocyst embryo and our duty to protect the individual human life.

I would argue that the lack of consensus is driven by a lack of widespread knowledge of the facts regarding the origins of human life on a cellular level and human life on a somatic and individual level. So the question of when does life begin, is better phrased "when does an individual human life begin." Some dogmatic individuals claim with the same certainty the Church opposed Galileo's claim that the earth is not the center of the universe, that an individual human life begins with the fertilization of the egg cell by the sperm cell. This is superstition, not science. The belief that an individual human being begins with the fertilization of the egg cell by the sperm cell is without basis in scientific fact or, for that matter, without basis in religious tradition.

All strategies to source human cells for the purposes of transplantation have their own unique ethical problems. Because developing embryonic and fetal cells and tissues are "young" and are still in the process of forming mature tissues, there has been considerable interest in obtaining these tissues for use in human medicine. However, the use of aborted embryo or fetal tissue raises numerous issues ranging from concerns over increasing the frequency of elected abortion to simple issues of maintaining quality controls standards in this hypothetical industry. Similarly, obtaining cells and tissues from living donors or cadavers is also not without ethical issues. For instance, an important question is, "Is it morally acceptable to keep "deceased" individuals on life support for long periods of time in order to harvest organs as they are needed?"

> **This is truly a matter of life and death.**

The implementation of ES-based technologies could address some of the ethical problems described above. First, it is important to note that the production of large numbers of human ES cells would not in itself cause these same concerns in accessing human embryonic or fetal tissue, since the resulting cells have the potential to be grown for very long periods of time. Using only a limited number of human embryos not used during in vitro fertilization procedures, could supply many millions of patients if the problem of histocompatibility could be resolved. Second, in the case of NT procedures, the patient may be at lower risk of complications in transplant rejection. Third, the only human cells used would be from the patient. Theoretically, the need to access tissue from other human beings could be reduced.

Sin by omission

Having knowledge of a means to dramatically improve the delivery of health care places a heavy burden on the shoulders of those who would actively impede ES and NT technology. The emphasis on the moral error of sin by omission is widely reflected in Western tradition traceable to Biblical tradition. In

Matthew chapter 25 we are told of the parable of the master who leaves talents of gold with his servants. One servant, for fear of making a mistake with what was given him, buries the talent in the ground. This servant, labeled "wicked and slothful" in the Bible, reminds us, that simple inaction, when we have been given a valuable asset, is not just a lack of doing good, but is in reality evil. There are times that it is not better to be safe than sorry.

Historically, the United States has a proud history of leading the free world in the bold exploration of new technologies. We did not hesitate to apply our best minds in an effort to allow a man to touch the moon. We were not paralyzed by the fear that like the tower of Babel, we were reaching for the heavens. But a far greater challenge stands before us. We have been given two talents of gold. The first, the human embryonic stem cell, the second, nuclear transfer technology. Shall we, like the good steward, take these gifts to mankind and courageously use them to the best of our abilities to alleviate the suffering of our fellow human being, or will we fail most miserably and bury these gifts in the earth? This truly is a matter of life and death. I urge you to stand courageously in favor of existing human life. The alternative is to inherit the wind.

10

Embryonic Stem Cell Research Is Not Ethical

Dennis P. Hollinger

Dennis P. Hollinger is vice provost, college pastor, and professor of Christian ethics at Messiah College in Grantham, Pennsylvania. He is also a fellow with the Center for Bioethics and Human Dignity and currently serves as an adjunct professor in the bioethics program at Trinity International University. His books include Choosing the Good: Christian Ethics in a Complex World. *He also serves as the coeditor for the series,* Critical Issues in Bioethics.

Embryonic stem cell research uses cells from the embryo's inner cell mass that give rise to each of the human body's many different tissue types. Supporters of stem cell research usually make one of two major arguments. First, they make a utilitarian argument that sacrificing a few embryos to use their stem cells for research is justified because the medical applications will help many suffering people. Second, supporters argue that the virtue of compassion for those who could benefit from stem cell research overrides any other ethical considerations about its use. Utilitarianism and appeals to compassion, so prominent in contemporary American culture, are dangerous. Instead of following God's directives, humans are relying on their subjective and emotional responses to make important decisions about stem cell research.

In the midst of the debate over using embryonic stem cells in research, a more fundamental issue has often been overlooked. It is a reality that will not only affect the outcome of this debate, but of numerous moral quandaries in the days ahead. It is the issue of our moral culture—that is, how we think about and seek to resolve moral issues. Our moral culture is ultimately more significant than is a given moral issue because it directly influences the decisions that are made regarding all such issues. It serves as the lens through which we understand much of life and our sense of goodness, justice and the morally right. It impacts not only individuals' thinking, but the larger cultural ethos and its perspectives on a myriad of moral issues.

If we listen closely to the moral discourse arguing that embryonic stem cells should be employed in medical research, we get a glimpse into the prevailing moral culture of our time. At its heart is a utilitarian calculus, combined with an unlimited emphasis on the virtue of compassion and undergirded by a worldview of what we might call "spiritualistic naturalism."

Utilitarian philosophy

In addition to being a conscious commitment of certain ethicists, utilitarianism is also a subconscious commitment of the masses and a powerful moral impetus that will likely shape thinking and action for years to come. Utilitarianism emerged in the nineteenth century as an attempt to establish the field of ethics as a scientific exercise distinct from religion or any worldview commitments. Contrasting their ethical system with the prevailing "principle ethics" of the day, [utilitarian philosophers] like Jeremy Bentham and John Stuart Mill argued that the foundation for ethics was consequences of a particular kind: namely, the greatest good (defined as happiness or pleasure) for the greatest number of people. In this formulation, ethics could actually be quantified and freed from dependence on any prior commitment to ethical norms (such as love, justice, or human dignity) or metaphysical outlooks, including religious ones. Here was an ethic for the entire society that could unite all peoples, whatever their religious or worldview commitments.

Supporters of stem cell research invoke utilitarianism

When we look at the arguments supporting the use of embryonic stem cells, they invariably incorporate utilitarian sentiments. Using both sophisticated and populist argumentation, proponents contend that the end result of sacrificing embryos to harvest their stem cells would be so overwhelmingly positive for a large number of suffering people that it must be the right thing to do. The moral calculus points to the alleged potential good of treating or healing illnesses such as Parkinson's disease, Alzheimer's disease, or diabetes. According to a commonly-heard argument, without the use of embryonic stem cells critical research cannot move forward, and the amelioration of human suffering and the saving of lives will be thwarted. The end goal of healing justifies the destruction of human embryos to procure stem cells. Healing is regarded as the "greatest good" which will usher in the most happiness or pleasure for the greatest number of people. Therefore, it should be pursued at the expense of embryonic life.

> *It is not at all evident why human happiness or pleasure for the greatest number of people should be regarded as the defining end of moral action.*

At the popular level the utilitarian argument is evident in the following statement by a 41-year-old man who has fought diabetes for 23 years: "It seems to me that it's an easy choice to make—take a shot at saving lives and making life easier for people." The utilitarian calculus is at the heart of a letter from the Association of American Medical Colleges (AAMC) to President Bush. While acknowledging that some people consider embryonic stem cell research to be wrong because of the ethical issues it raises, the AAMC states, "We are persuaded otherwise by what we believe is an equally compelling ethical consideration, namely that it would be tragic to waste the unique potential afforded by embryonic stem cells, destined to be discarded in any case, to alleviate human suffering and enhance the quality of life."

Critical objections to utilitarianism

Utilitarianism, however, has always faced some critical problems and objections. First, it is not at all evident why human happiness or pleasure for the greatest number of people should be regarded as the defining end of moral action. Utilitarianism purports to rely upon an amoral criterion in weighing the consequences of human action, but happiness is hardly an amoral criterion. Second, this approach to ethics argues that the sought end (happiness or pleasure for the greatest number of people) justifies the means of achieving that end. The problem with this is that some means to obtaining this goal are clearly morally suspect. In the late 18th century, [scholar] Thomas Malthus justified the dying off of large numbers of poor and hungry people for the good end of curbing population growth. Utilitarians assume that no means are problematic as long as the end result justifies them. And third, utilitarianism has to make some difficult factual judgments when it comes to calculating the greatest good for the greatest number. It assumes an objectivity in making this assessment. With regard to embryonic stem cell research, it assumes that embryonic stem cells will prove to have significant therapeutic value; however, this is still only a projection (though not without some warrant given the animal research done thus far). Also of interest is the fact that proponents tend to downplay the potential of adult stem cells, which have already proven to be therapeutic in clinical trials. This should tell us something about the objectivity (or lack thereof) of weighing consequences.

The virtue of compassion

The second major approach to defending the use of human embryos for harvesting stem cells extols the virtue of compassion. Virtue ethics tends to focus less on moral actions and more on internal moral dispositions or character, from which actions naturally flow. For a number of ethical issues today (e.g., abortion, physician-assisted suicide, and homosexuality), compassion as a virtue has become the moral trump card. It is heralded as the virtue above all virtues, for to subjugate compassion to any other moral claim is to exhibit an insensitivity toward and a lack of empathy for others.

With regard to embryonic stem cell research, the public campaign for federal funding was carried primarily by actors such as Christopher Reeve and Michael J. Fox, who utilized media blitzes to appeal to people's passions. Seeing Reeve in his wheelchair hardly evoked solid ethical reflection, but instead moved the masses to feel compassion for him. A letter [appearing in the *Washington Post* on February 21, 2001,] to President Bush, signed by a group of Nobel Laureates urging funding for research with human embryos, exalted the virtue of compassion over all other values. While it "recognized the legitimate ethical issues raised by this research," it also asserted that "it would be tragic to waste this opportunity to pursue the work that could potentially alleviate human suffering." Alleviating human suffering strikes a chord in American culture, for in this "happiness-oriented land" we seek above all else to wipe away pain and discomfort. Thus, as one scientist put it, it really is quite simple to decide whether to protect a "mass of cells in a dish" or to protect a "43-year-old father of two."

Ethics cannot be built on emotions

While appeals to compassion are becoming increasingly common in public debate, regarding compassion as the moral trump card is problematic. [In his book, *Begotton or Made*, professor] Oliver O'Donovan of Oxford University rightly reminds us that the virtue of compassion can never stand alone. "Compassion is the virtue of being moved to action by the sight of suffering. . . . It is a virtue that circumvents thought, since it prompts us immediately to action. It is a virtue that presupposes that an answer has already been found to the question, 'What needs to be done?'" The appeal to compassion overlooks divine givens in which there are inherent meaning and worth within the created realities of this world. Compassion, conversely, brings its own meaning to the suffering situation in such a way that all else becomes secondary, for it appeals primarily to our emotions. [The Greek philosopher] Socrates was certainly right when he warned us that ethics cannot be built on emotions—not because they are unimportant, but because they alone cannot be trusted to discover the human right and good within the perils of human finitude and fallenness.

> *When set apart from the moral givens of a loving, gracious Creator, compassion will lead us to the abyss of moral nihilism.*

In the final analysis, compassion as the moral trump card is one more example of how our culture seeks to determine what is right, good and just on the basis of what will secure self-enhancement or self-actualization. Of course, compassion should indeed be reflected in the habits and actions of all persons. We can never be indifferent to human need and must in fact seek ethically legitimate solutions to disease and suffering. However, when set apart from the moral givens of a loving, gracious Creator, compassion will lead us to the abyss of moral nihilism.

Spiritualistic naturalism: an American worldview

Underlying all moral principles and virtues is a larger narrative or worldview. Humans never develop their ethical norms in a vacuum, but always in relation to their understandings of transcendence and human nature, perspectives on what is fundamentally wrong in the world, beliefs about how that wrong should be rectified (i.e., salvation), and perceptions of the course of human history. How we put "our world" together invariably determines which moral principles or virtues we espouse and which ones we reject.

> *The well-being of human embryos has for many taken a backseat to the greatest happiness of the whole.*

In contemporary American culture, we seem increasingly to be reflecting a worldview that might be termed "spiritualistic naturalism." Though institutional religion may be on the decline, spirituality seems to be flourishing. Indeed many people today say they are not religious, but are deeply spiritual. However, their spirituality is often not grounded in a strong sense of transcendence and divine givens. Rather, it is, as sociologist Robert Wuthnow puts it, "a new spirituality of seeking . . . [in which people] increasingly negotiate among competing glimpses of the sacred, seeking partial knowledge and practical wisdom." In their search for fleeting moments of sacred encounter, today's spiritualists tend toward a fragmented worldview which bears little resemblance to classical supernaturalism—which holds that God not only created the world, but provided meaning, significance and content to it. There is in the classical theistic worldview a sense that God has spoken and that we must therefore respond by seeking life's full meaning and the morally good.

In contrast, spiritualistic naturalism functions without recourse to moral and worldview givens, seeking instead experiences that engender a sense of spirituality with minimal content, essence, and direction. In spiritualistic naturalism, meaning is self-made and moral direction is derived from within a self that defines the good, the right, and the just. Subjectivity takes the place of providential design and direction. It is a naturalism in that functional transcendence plays no meaningful role in the moral direction of people's lives, but it is a spiritualism in that spiritual experiences that evoke a sense that people are not alone in this world—and that enhance their selfhood and compassion for others—are sought. Utilitarianism flows from the naturalistic side of this worldview and compassion from its spiritualistic side.

Thus, in the moral discourse about embryonic stem cells the utilitarian calculus and the virtue of compassion emerge out of this particular worldview. The well-being of human embryos has for many taken a backseat to the greatest happiness of the whole, precisely because of an ethos that minimizes inherent meaning in life and the existence of God-given directives. Compassion has become the moral trump card because it is an emotional response that reflects the "fleeting moments" spirituality of our time.

Western worldview often renders moral issues amoral

Spiritualistic naturalism may well be the emerging worldview of Western culture. Unlike old naturalisms it seeks a spiritual ethos, albeit one in which God is functionally absent in the formation of moral character and the adjudication of moral decisions. Because of its spirituality, this form of naturalism tends to blind us to its true reality—a worldview in which the human subject reigns supreme and becomes the ultimate arbiter of the good, the just, and the right. It is this worldview which tends to render moral issues amoral, as when Panayiotis Zavos, the aspiring cloner, told *Time* magazine [February 19, 2001], "Ethics is a wonderful word, but we need to look beyond the ethical issues here [with regard to cloning]. It's not an ethical issue. It's a medical issue. We have a duty here. Some people need this to complete the life cycle, to reproduce." Similar sentiments have led the masses of our culture to embrace the use of embryonic stem cells for the greater good—out of a sense of compassion—precisely because there are no perceived providential renderings to order our lives.

This is the ethos in which we now find ourselves. We must recognize it for what it is and bear witness to a better way.

11

More Legislation Is Needed to Regulate the Genetic Engineering of Animals

Andrew B. Perzigian

Andrew B. Perzigian is a contributor to the Animal Legal and Historical Web Center, a Web site published by the Detroit College of Law at Michigan State University. The Web site is an electronic library of law reviews and articles about the most recent changes in animal law.

Proponents of genetic engineering argue that animal genetic research will produce many benefits for society. For example, genetically engineered cows can produce higher quality meat and milk. Scientists can use specially engineered animals to study treatments for diseases such as cancer, AIDS, and hypertension. Genetic engineering in the form of cloning can even be used to save endangered species. Critics of animal engineering, however, argue that altering animals for medical research is a cruel and inhumane denial of basic animal rights. They also say that releasing genetically modified animals into the wild would threaten natural ecosystems. Furthermore, they point out that cloning endangered species does not address the underlying cause of species extinction: human infringement on nature. While both sides make valid arguments, genetic experimentation with animals seems inevitable. The United States and the European Union must therefore create stronger legislation to regulate biotechnology.

With the advent and rapid development of genetic engineering technology, the animal rights movement is currently facing one of its greatest challenges and dilemmas. This technology is capable of efficiently creating multi-cellular, transgenic animals. Like any technological breakthrough, genetic engineering brings with it as much promise as it does uncertainty, and so, the value judgments we make regarding the direction and scope of this technology are sure to have far reaching implications. Such value judgments, though routed in science, involve legal dilemmas as well. Importantly, the use of patents as a means of protecting and owning genetically engineered animals and species figures to be one of the more prominent battlegrounds in the emerging debate on genetic engineering.

Transgenic animals are animals that have specific traits from another plant or animal genetically engineered into them. Unlike controlled breeding, which is confined to the genetic material contained in a single species, genetic engineering permits an almost limitless scope of modification and introduction of otherwise foreign genetic material. Traditional methods, which could only breed with two closely related species, produced offspring that carried a diverse amalgamation of each of its parent's traits. In contrast, modern genetic engineers are able to introduce completely foreign genetic material, from both plants and animals, into another plant or animal. This permits only the desired traits, and not the host of other traits common from crossbreeding, to be effectively introduced into new, transgenic animal species. Eventually genetic engineers will be able to manufacture genes that nature has never produced. Regardless, genetic engineering is currently able to create whole organisms that are not natural to the planet, and whose specific genetic make-up is as much a result of human manipulation as it is natural selection. Thus, the ethical, cultural, and environmental implications involve issues of the greatest magnitude and importance.

Transgenic animals in the agricultural industry

[According to writer Carrie Walter,] transgenic farm animals can be created that "are better able to resist disease, have increased growth performance, and have better reproductive traits." For instance, transgenic salmon, that grow larger and at a faster rate than natural varieties, have already been created and farmed. Another common use of genetic engineering technology is the use of bovine growth hormone in dairy cows to increase their milk production. In the future, transgenic sheep can be created to produce better wool and cows can be engineered to more efficiently convert grain into higher quality milk and meat.

> *Animals are . . . engineered to produce therapeutic drugs that are otherwise impossible to replicate in the laboratory setting.*

Biotechnology is equally poised to transform factory farming with the creation of transgenic farm animals that are created to be non-sentient, without the ability to experience pleasure or feel pain. By removing the "stress" gene from livestock, genetic engineers may render animals non-sentient and thus outside the concern of much animal rights ideology. [Environmental Protection Agency legal analyst Jon Owens asserts that] making animals unaware of their suffering could provide a powerful argument against allegations of mistreatment, inhumane practices, and result in a great "diminution" of the animal rights movement's "moral imperative to feel for animals." Owens asserts that this technology would leave the modified animals with the "same status as a rock, which earns no protection under the movement's philosophy." Peter Singer, one of the great animal rights theorists in modern times, agrees, believing that such technology would actually be the "triumph" of his moral philosophy, that it would realize a great reduction in the human causes of animal suffering. Of course, this process would not be generally applicable for the biomedical community since animal-based research often relies to a large extent on measuring the sentient reactions of animals to drugs, household products, psychological stimuli and physical harm.

This potential may be quickly outdated with the advent of animaless meat. Genetic engineers will likely be able to do this, to create the meat, or flesh of animals without creating the whole being. This could potentially eradicate the suffering of agricultural animals, the huge environmental damage caused by factory farming, and it could provide leaner, more nutritious meat than what is naturally produced as a result of traditional and close confinement agricultural methods.

Using transgenic animals as research models

Genetic engineering is fast altering the biomedical research world. By creating animal models that express only desired traits, biomedical research is made faster, more accurate, less expensive, and at the expense of fewer animal lives. For instance, when specific genes are removed from animals, researchers are then able to determine the exact function of that gene by observing the various biological changes the transgenic animal model exhibits. Researchers are also able to study a hereditary human disease, like breast cancer, by injecting cancer-causing genes (oncogenes) into non-human mammals. This was the case for the first transgenic animal patent, the "oncomouse," secured by Harvard researchers in 1988. Because the oncomouse had a propensity for developing breast cancer, researchers have been able to better understand carcinogens and their replication into cancerous cells.

Various other diseases, from hypertension, to AIDS, Down's syndrome, Alzheimer's disease, high cholesterol, anemia, and hepatitis B, are likewise being studied through the use of genetically engineered animal models. Transgenic animals have made research of such diseases more accurate, less expensive and faster, while at the same time permitting such results with the use of fewer individual animals in any given study.

GE animals produce medicine

Animals are also engineered to produce therapeutic drugs that are otherwise impossible to replicate in the laboratory setting. Transgenic animals, like goats, sheep, and cattle, have been engineered to produce large amounts of complex human proteins in their milk. Such proteins can be especially beneficial for hemophiliacs (clotting factors in proteins), AIDS and cancer patients with depleted bone marrow, and those suffering from emphysema and various other lung problems.

Prior to such technology, animals (mostly pigs and sheep) have been used "as factories for producing such proteins as human growth hormone and insulin," [according to Carrie Walter]. Typically, such animals had to be slaughtered before such proteins could be derived. By engineering these animals to release these and other proteins in their milk, the mass production of high quality therapeutic drugs is made less costly, easier to manufacture, and at the expense of fewer animal lives than what was formerly the case.

Researchers are also genetically modifying animals so that they produce genes able to be used in human gene therapy. For instance, transgenic, albino mice have been cured of albinism with the use of such therapy, and the hope of a human cure is thus much greater. Finally, much research has been forwarded with the goal of creating "near human" organs inside transgenic animals. Such organs, researchers hope, will provide a more viable source of livers, kidneys, and hearts for humans in need of transplants.

Cloning endangered species

The World Wildlife Fund estimates that within 30 years, 20% of the earth's biodiversity will be lost to extinction, almost entirely as a result of human causes. A different species becomes extinct every fifteen minutes, amounting to 35,000 species per year. As Chief Justice Burger remarked in *TVA v. Hill*, the importance of individual endangered species and their supporting populations is "incalculable." This potentially irreversible result of human exploitation and depletion of the earth's resources has found an incremental solution in genetic engineering technology. Since the 1997 birth of Dolly, the first fully cloned mammal derived from adult cells, cloning technology has been used for the renewal of endangered species populations and the resurrection of species already extinct. In Iowa, an adult cow gave birth to a gaur, an endangered species of ox from South America, whose embryo had been cloned and implanted in the mother cow. And, efforts in Australia are currently underway to clone a Tasmanian tiger that has been extinct for nearly 100 years. Around the world, scientists are searching for intact woolly mammoth DNA in hopes of resurrecting this species, a hotly debated use of genetic engineering technology since the earth has been without the woolly mammoth for nearly 10,000 years.

Regardless of this sort of controversial use of bioengineering technology, cloning endangered, or recently extinct species may provide many benefits. Significantly, cloning would help support endangered species populations, at least in zoos and laboratories, with a greater genetic diversity and thus a more sustainable population for reintroduction into the wild. Also, scientists could clone endangered species from frozen DNA, which is stored throughout America's zoos, thereby permitting otherwise "lost" genes to be reintroduced to the endangered species gene pool. Finally, species like tigers and pandas, who are notoriously difficult to breed in captivity, could also be cloned and their populations thereby preserved more efficiently than is otherwise possible in controlled breeding circumstances.

The potential risks of animal genetics

While genetic engineering is quickly making an indelible mark on society, and its promise is great, there are a number of concerns about the ramifications that genetic engineering has for society and the environment. Environmental advocates and animal rights groups are often the loudest voices in opposition. For each solution that genetic engineering claims to solve, there are inherent risks. In general, opponents of genetic engineering assert that such technology creates a huge diminution in the standing of animals, leaving them as nothing more than "test tubes with tails," only of benefit for the exploitive practices of factory farming, and drug and organ manufacturing. There are both real and potential risks associated with biotechnology and its manipulation of animal genetics.

> *The World Wildlife Fund estimates that within 30 years, 20% of the earth's biodiversity will be lost to extinction.*

Transgenic agricultural animals pose a number of threats. Many argue that creating more efficient farm animals will cause a cessation of selective breeding, thereby lessening the genetic diversity of such animals. This could make whole herds susceptible to new strains of infectious diseases. Others argue that transgenic farm animals are far more likely to endure greater suffering than what is already experienced on factory farms. For instance, when the USDA [U.S. Department of Agriculture] implanted a human growth hormone into a pig, the unfortunate result were pigs who ended up "bowlegged, cross-eyed, arthritic, and had dysfunctional immune systems that made them susceptible to pneumonia," [according to Iowa State University professor Gary Comstock]. Likewise, dairy cows, who are commonly injected with recumbent bovine growth hormone (rBgh) to increase their rate of milk production, are much more likely to suffer from udder disease. Transgenic animals, if released or escape into natural, wild environments, pose an enormous threat to native animal populations and the overall balance of the ecosystem. [Antibiotechnology activist Jeremy Rifkin argues] that any leak of genetically engineered organism into the wild is "tantamount to playing ecological roulette." This is so because of the complexity of biochemical functions, about which very little is known regarding the precise function that each species serves within the greater ecosystem. Artificially created species, the argument goes, are unsustainable because they are not a part of the "web of highly synchronized relationships" that have evolved over millions of years. For instance, in a study done at Purdue University, scientists calculated that if 60 genetically engineered salmon escaped into a native, natural population of 60,000, it would take only 40 generations for the wild salmon to be completely wiped out. There is no way of predicting the exact effects of transgenic animals on the environment, and because studies indicate that unnatural genetic manipulation poses a devastating threat to wild environments, opponents of genetic engineering believe that overconfidence must be tempered and that genetically engineered solutions are no answer for the world's current agricultural challenges. [Ned Hettinger, author of *Patenting Life: Biotechnology, Intellectual Property, and Environmental Ethics*, states that], "even in the cases where no adverse impacts on the ecological functioning of natural ecosystems occur, the mere presence of introduced genes and genetically-altered organisms degrades these ecosystems by diminishing the naturalness or wildness of these ecosystems."

Natural rights of animals

Creating transgenic farm animals is considered not only threatening to natural ecosystems, but also devastating as a form of mistreatment. This concept centers upon the notion of species integrity, the idea that every animal, whether owned by humans or not, has a natural right to have its genetic code left intact and untouched. This notion of integrity, though calling for a complete ban on transgenic animals, centers mostly on the use of biotechnology on agricultural animals because of the widespread threat such animals pose to natural ecosystems.

Apart from a complete ban on transgenic animals, the species integrity argument serves as an important consideration with regard to agricultural animals that are engineered insentient. Because this use of biotechnology is so new, few scholarly reactions have been published in regard to it. At minimum, such technology helps to substantiate the belief that animals are sentient, that they are conscious beings deserving not only of protection, but deep respect and thoughtful consideration. Likewise, if such technology is eventually practiced and utilized, the culpable act of killing, or mistreatment and cruelty of animals will still exist. Nothing will have been done to address this underlying dilemma.

This is true because sentience is not the only aspect that separates animals from, say, plants or rocks. Insentient animals, presumably, would still experience the world in a number of ways beyond their judgments of pain or pleasure—by thinking, communicating, moving, seeing, touching, tasting, nurturing their young, among others. Such animals would still demand greater consideration than plants or rocks. Potentially, genetic engineering animals to be senseless to mistreatment might only exacerbate what is really the focus of the call for animal rights—the belief that mistreating animals is cruel, abusive and wrong and that no amount of technology or distance from the slaughterhouses can erase complicity.

Ned Hettinger, one of the few scholars to comment briefly on this use of bioengineering, remarks,

> A future where descendents of chickens are wired to the floor, connected to input tubes, and do not mind because their sentience has been biotechnologically removed is not a pleasing picture of what biotechnology may bring. There exists a significant burden of justification against the production of such monstrous transformations of living beings into mechanical, artificial modes of existence. Prima facie, biotechnology should not be used to impoverish creatures, to strip away their capacities, or to diminish the richness of their lives.

On the other hand, the potential for biotechnology to create flesh without the animal seems to be a far less heinous proposition. Although there is also very little scholarship involving this topic, it seems that such technology might actually solve many of the problems that animal rights advocates and environmentalists see with the use of sentient animals for food, medicine, and clothing. Of course, there might still be debate regarding what exactly constitutes an animal and too what extent the presence of animal DNA or animal cellular structure demands protection under the animal rights movement.

Increased suffering for research animals

Creating more efficient research animals, though potentially a means of reducing the absolute number of individual animals used for experiment, threatens to actually increase the suffering experienced by research animals. One of the more common uses of bioengineering is for the purposeful creation of animals who are either diseased or afflicted with a predisposition to develop a fatal, genetic disease. Such research animals are purposefully created to suffer. The entire population of genetically engineered research animals exist in bodies whose inevitable fate is constant pain and unnaturally rapid deterioration. [According to Henry J. Miller, author of *Patenting Animals*] these animals are specifically "tailored to be hypersensitive to a variety of carcinogens, mutagens, taratogens, or other poisons." Their lives, many would argue, are a nightmare, worse than even their human counterparts, purposefully tailored to experience our greatest maladies behind wire cages, underneath microscopes, and inside laboratories. If anything, engineering animals to be more efficient research tools, to accentuate their sentience for the benefit of the human predicament alone, only perpetuates the same concerns that animal rights organizations have always held—that research animals are abused, badly mistreated, and without even the most basic of rights.

Underlying causes of species extinction remain

While cloning endangered species may provide a short-term, partial solution to the modern extinction crisis, it by no means addresses all the issues of conservation biology and the need to protect both the endangered species and the habitats that support them. All animals, including endangered species, serve hugely important functions within their ecosystems. While only a few animals act as lynchpins in the overall sustainability of human dominated ecosystems, there is much to be understood about all the subtle bio-chemical purposes that each species serves within the whole.

Cloning endangered species does little to address the underlying causes pushing such species so near to extinction. The World Wildlife Fund reports that the greatest threats to endangered species are a result of human settlement, deforestation, water, soil and air pollution, climate changes due to overuse of fossil fuels, and poaching to supply international markets with rare animal parts. These threats still loom large even with the possibility of cloning. Most opponents agree [with Robert F. Bloomquist, who writes about legal perspectives on cloning] that cloning endangered species should only be implemented "as a last, desperate attempt to try and preserve a given species," not as strategy for their protection.

> **❝** *Creating transgenic farm animals is considered not only threatening to natural ecosystems, but also devastating as a form of mistreatment.* **❞**

Since cloning animals is a hugely expensive procedure, opponents also argue that cloning endangered species should not be a means of cutting into the already stretched funds needed to maintain critical habitats and overall biodiversity. The primary goals of biodiversity are not solely for the protection of the most threatened species, but for the maintenance of a thriving pool of genetically diverse, naturally selected organisms that are specifically adapted to their given environments. Cloning technology can exist within these goals, but it is neither a complete solution nor a feasible alternative to habitat preservation and the real threats causing a contraction of Earth's biodiversity. . . .

We must take action

Bioengineering technology, used as a means of cloning whole animals and for creating new breeds of transgenic animal species, promises as many triumphs as it clouded with great uncertainty and backlash. Proponents of the technology assert that transgenic animals (and plants) may one day help solve many of our modern day challenges in life; from starvation and ill health, to environmental degradation and the modern extinction crisis. Critics believe that bioengineering brings with it greater risks than it does alleviate current problems. They argue that genetic engineering threatens to increase animal suffering and decrease species integrity, while at the same time creating a potentially devastating impact on the balance and sustainability of Earth's ecosystem.

While each side's assertions may be equally valid, there is no doubt that genetic engineering will continue to expand the frontiers of cloning and the creation of transgenic animals well into the future. Both the United States' and the EU's legal systems have been slow to respond with legislation specifically regulating biotechnology, and each have permitted their patent law to provide a supportive ground for genetic engineering research and development to continue with great incentive. Although human cloning is proscribed, little is in the way of genetic engineers from creating vast arrays of transgenic agricultural and research animals in both the United States and the EU. How this technology will affect human populations and how it will be perceived by the general public and animal rights groups alike, largely remains to be seen. One thing is for sure, we must not sit complacently by as this technology rapidly changes the fabric of our existence from the inside out. We must not wait and see what the effects are. We must form educated opinions, inspire legislative regulation, and hope that whatever direction that bioengineering takes, is a positive step towards decreased animal suffering, increased environmental sustainability, and an overall compassionate regard for the earth and its precious life.

Organizations to Contact

The editors have compiled the following list of organizations concerned with the issues debated in this book. The descriptions are derived from materials provided by the organizations. All have publications or information available for interested readers. The list was compiled on the date of publication of the present volume; names, addresses, phone and fax numbers, and e-mail addresses may change. Be aware that many organizations take several weeks or longer to respond to inquiries, so allow as much time as possible.

Agricultural Biotechnology Council (ABC)
PO Box 38 589, London, SW1AWE, UK
+44 (0) 207 898 9103 • fax: +44 (0) 207 898 9252
e-mail: Enquires@abcinformation.org
Web site: www.abcinformation.org

The Agricultural Biotechnology Council is a London-based organization created by several agricultural biotechnology companies to offer information and education services and to address concerns about foods that have been genetically engineered. The companies involved in this organization include Bayer CropScience, BASF, Dow AgroSciences, DuPont, Monsanto, and Syngenta. ABC is committed to the safe and responsible development of agricultural biotechnology. Its Web site has many downloadable reports concerning genetically modified organisms (GMOs) and a downloadable book titled *GM Crops—Understanding the Issues*.

Alliance for Aging Research
2021 K St. NW, Suite 305, Washington, DC 20006
(202) 293-2856 • fax: (202) 785-8574
e-mail: info@agingresearch.org • Web site: www.agingresearch.org

The Alliance for Aging Research encourages public and private sector research toward newer and better treatments that have the potential to improve the health and independence of Americans as they age. The alliance fights for federal legislation that will advance medical breakthroughs, encourages greater funding for the National Institutes of Health, and brings visibility and support to aging research. Its Web site contains educational materials on a variety of subjects, including therapeutic cloning and biomedical research, and information on how to get involved and make a difference.

American Genetic Association (AGA)
PO Box 257, Buckeystown, MD 21717-0257
(301) 695-9292
e-mail: agajoh@mail.ncifcrf.gov
Web site: www.theaga.org/overview.html

Formerly the American Breeders Association, the American Genetic Association publishes genetic research in fields such as genomic diversity, comparative genetics, species conservation, molecular evolution, and plant and animal domestication.

Biotechnology Industry Organization (BIO)
1625 K St. NW, Suite 1100, Washington, DC 20006
(202) 857-0244
Web site: www.bio.org

The Biotechnology Industry Organization represents biotechnology companies, academic institutions, state biotechnology centers, and related organizations that support the use of biotechnology in agriculture, health care, and other fields. BIO works to educate the public about biotechnology and responds to concerns about the safety and ethics of genetic engineering and related technologies. Its Web site includes an introductory guide to biotechnology as well as links to other biotechnology Web sites, press releases, and position papers on bioethics, food and agriculture, and similar topics.

Center for Bioethics
3401 Market St., Suite 320, Philadelphia, PA 19104-3319
(215) 898-7136 • fax: (215) 573-3036
Web site: www.bioethics.upenn.edu

The Center for Bioethics is a world-renowned educational and research facility focusing on the ethical practice of life sciences and medicine. Its newsletter *PennBioethics* is available at its Web site. The center's Web site also includes the Penn High School Bioethics Project, which offers online tutoring, bioethics homework help, a bioethics forum, a video entitled *Designer Babies*, and pertinent links to further information about genetic engineering.

Council for Responsible Genetics (CRG)
5 Upland Rd., Suite 3, Cambridge, MA 02140
(617) 868-0870 • fax: (617) 491-5344
e-mail: crg@gene-watch.org • Web site: www.gene-watch.org

The Council for Responsible Genetics is a national nonprofit organization of scientists and others devoted to encouraging public debate about the social, ethical, and environmental implications of new genetic technologies. It works to provide the public with clear and understandable information on genetic innovations so that people can participate in decision making about genetic technology and its implementation. Material on CRG's Web site includes a petition titled, "No Patents on Life," a position paper on manipulation of the human germ line, and news alerts.

Dolan DNA Learning Center (DNALC)
334 Main St., Cold Spring Harbor, NY 11724
(516) 367-5170 • fax: (516) 367-3043
e-mail: dnalc@cshl.edu • Web site: www.dnalc.org

The Dolan DNA Learning Center is the world's first science center devoted entirely to public genetics education and is an operating unit of Cold Spring Harbor Laboratory, an important center for molecular genetics research. DNALC provides students from fifth through twelfth grades with hands-on laboratory experience and offers them educational opportunities that are unavailable in their own schools. Its multidisciplinary staff has experience in elementary, secondary, and collegiate instruction. Dolan DNA Learning Center serves as a clearinghouse for information on DNA science, genetic medicine, and biotechnology, and provides a forum for public discussion of the personal, social, and ethical implications of DNA science. This organization offers week-long, hands-on genetic workshops for middle and high school students.

Food Ethics Council
39-41 Surrey St., Brighton, BN1 3PB, UK
+44 (0) 1273 766 654 • fax: +44 (0) 1273 766 653
e-mail: info@foodethicscouncil.org
Web site: www.foodethicscouncil.org

The Food Ethics Council is an independent organization that advocates the development of a food system that is secure, sustainable, just, and humane. The council encourages interaction between businesspeople, policy makers, and consumers. Its Web site offers reports on genetically modified foods based on in-house research.

Genetically Engineered Food Alert (GEFA)
1200 Eighteenth St. NW, Fifth Fl., Washington, DC 20036
(800) 390-3373 • fax: (800) 390-4751
3435 Wilshire Blvd., #380, Los Angeles, CA 90010
(213) 251-3680 • fax: (213) 251-3699
Web site: www.gefoodalert.org

Genetically Engineered Food Alert is a coalition of seven organizations committed to the testing and labeling of genetically engineered food. These organizations include Public Interest Research Group, National Environmental Trust, Institute for Agriculture and Trade Policy, Organic Consumers Association, Friends of the Earth, the Center for Food Safety, and Pesticide Action Network of North America. GEFA encourages an active campaign against genetically engineered (GE) foods. Its Web site contains many reports, articles, and press releases about the issues of GE foods.

GeneWatch UK
The Mill House
Manchester Rd., Tideswell, Buxton, Derbyshire, SK 17 8LN, UK
+44 (0) 1298 871 898 • fax: +44 (0) 1298 872 531
e-mail: mail@genewatch.org • Web site: www.genewatch.org

GeneWatch works to ensure that genetic technologies are developed and used in a way that promotes human health, protects the environment, and respects human rights and the interests of animals. This organization promotes education to increase public understanding of genetic technologies and encourages public involvement in the decisions that are made about how genetic technologies are used.

Greenpeace USA
702 H St. NW, Suite 300, Washington, DC 20001
(202) 462-1177 • fax: (202) 462-4507
e-mail: greenpeace.usa@wdc.greenpeace.org
Web site: www.greenpeaceusa.org

Greenpeace is a nonprofit organization that advocates immediate measures to end threats posed by genetic engineering. Greenpeace also opposes all patents on plants, animals, and humans, as well as patents on their genes. The organization conducts research, lobbies for various causes, and carries out media campaigns.

Kennedy Institute of Ethics

Georgetown University, Box 571212, Washington, DC 20057-1212
(202) 687-8099 • fax: (202) 687-8089
e-mail: kicourse@georgetown.edu
Web site: http://kennedyinstitute.georgetown.edu

The Kennedy Institute of Ethics is a teaching and research center offering ethical perspectives on major policy issues. The institute also houses the most extensive library of bioethics in the world, the National Reference Center for Bioethics Literature. It runs a high school bioethics curriculum project featuring a high school human genome program. Its Web site features a virtual tour of the University of Washington Genome Center.

National Center for Biotechnology Information (NCBI)

National Library of Medicine, Bldg. 3A, Bethesda, MD 20894
(301) 496-2475 • fax: (301) 480-9241
e-mail: info@ncbi.nlm.nih.gov • Web site: www.ncbi.nih.gov

Operated by the National Library of Medicine, NCBI is a national resource for molecular biology information. Its quarterly newsletter *NCBI News* is available on its Web site, which also offers a downloadable and printable collection of articles titled *Genes and Disease* summarizing over eighty genetic disorders and their mutations. The site also contains a map of the twenty-four chromosomes and the diseases associated with each of them.

National Human Genome Research Institute (NHGRI)

9000 Rockville Pike, Bethesda, MD 20892
(301) 402-0911 • fax: (301) 402-0837
Web site: www.nhgri.nih.gov

Sponsored by the National Institutes of Health, the federal government's primary agency for the support of biomedical research, NHGRI heads the Human Genome Project, the federally funded effort to map all human genes. Information about the Human Genome Project, including its ethical, legal, and social implications, is available at NHGRI's Web site.

Nuffield Council on Bioethics

28 Bedford Sq., London, WC1B 3JS, UK
+44 (0) 20 7681 9619 • fax: +44 (0) 20 7637 1712
e-mail: bioethics@nuffieldfoundation.org
Web site: www.nuffieldbioethics.org

The Nuffield Council on Bioethics works to identify, examine, and report on the ethical questions raised by recent advances in biological and medical research. It also seeks to play a role in policy making and stimulating debate about bioethics. The Nuffield Council has published ten major reports on the ethical issues associated with genetic screening, ownership of tissue, xenotransplantation, genetics and mental disorders, genetically modified crops, stem cell therapy, DNA patenting, ethics in pharmacogenics, and genetics and human behavior.

President's Council on Bioethics
1801 Pennsylvania Ave. NW, Suite 700, Washington, DC 20006
(202) 296-4669
e-mail: info@bioethics.gov • Web site: http://bioethics.gov

Created by President George W. Bush on November 28, 2001, the council's purpose is to advise the president on bioethical issues resulting from advances in the biomedical science and technology industries. The President's Council explores policy issues and their consequences, provides a forum for national discussion of bioethical issues and promotes education and understanding of these issues. The council studies such subjects as embryonic stem cell research, assisted reproduction, cloning, and uses of human genetic technologies. Reports, transcripts, and working papers on many aspects of biotechnology are available on the council's Web site. In addition, the Web site contains the transcript of the book, *Being Human: Readings from the President's Council on Bioethics.*

U.S. Department of Agriculture (USDA)
Animal and Plant Health Inspection Service (APHIS)
Fourteenth and Independence Ave. SW, Washington, DC 20250
e-mail: john.t.turner@usda.gov
Web site: www.aphis.usda.gov/biotechnology

The USDA is one of three federal agencies, along with the Environmental Protection Agency (EPA) and the Food and Drug Administration (FDA), primarily responsible for regulating biotechnology in the United States. The USDA's Animal and Plant Health Inspection Service (APHIS) conducts research on the safety of genetically engineered organisms, helps form government policy on agricultural biotechnology, and provides information to the public about these technologies. The APHIS Web site includes policy statements on biotechnology, a description of the role of the USDA and its agencies in regulating agricultural biotechnology, and research reports, including "Impacts of Adopting Genetically Engineered Crops in the United States."

The Wellcome Trust
The Wellcome Building, 183 Euston Rd., London, NW1 2BE, UK
+44 (0) 20 7611 8888 • fax: +44 (0) 20 7611 8545
e-mail: genome@wellcome.zc.uk
Web site: www.wellcome.ac.uk/en/genome/aboutthissite.html

The Wellcome Trust promotes medical research to improve human and animal health. The Wellcome Trust also works to raise public awareness of the medical, ethical, and social implications of research and promote dialogue among scientists, the public, and policy makers. Its Web site includes a historical account and current information about the Human Genome Project.

Bibliography

Books

Pierre Baldi	*The Shattered Self: The End of Natural Evolution.* Cambridge: Massachusetts Institute of Technology, 2001.
Michael C. Brannigan	*Ethical Issues in Human Cloning.* New York: Seven Bridges, 2001.
British Medical Association	*Biotechnology Weapons and Humanity.* Amsterdam: Harwood, 1999.
Arthur Caplan	*Due Consideration: Controversy in the Age of Medical Miracles.* New York: John Wiley, 1998.
Ruth Chadwick, ed.	*The Concise Encyclopedia of the Ethics of New Technologies.* San Diego: Academic Press, 2001.
Michael W. Fox	*Beyond Evolution: The Genetically Altered Future of Plants, Animals, the Earth . . . and Humans.* New York: Lyons, 1999.
Michael W. Fox	*Bringing Life to Ethics: Global Bioethics for a Humane Society.* Albany: State University of New York Press, 2001.
Francis Fukuyama	*Our Posthuman Future: Consequences of the Biotechnology Revolution.* New York: Farrar, Straus and Giroux, 2002.
Anita Guerrini	*Experimenting with Humans and Animals: From Galen to Animal Rights.* Baltimore: Johns Hopkins University Press, 2003.
Kathleen Hart	*Eating in the Dark: America's Experiment with Genetically Engineered Food.* New York: Pantheon, 2002.
Suzanne Holland, Karen Lebacqz, and Laurie Zoloth, eds.	*The Human Embryonic Stem Cell Debate: Science, Ethics, and Public Policy.* Cambridge: Massachusetts Institute of Technology, 2001.
Paul F. Lurquin	*The Green Phoenix: A History of Genetically Modified Plants.* New York: Columbia University Press, 2001.
Paul F. Lurquin	*High Tech Harvest: Understanding Genetically Modified Food Plants.* Boulder, CO: Westview, 2002.
Glenn McGee	*The Perfect Baby: Parenthood in the New World of Cloning and Genetics.* Lanham, MD: Rowman & Littlefield, 2000.

Glenn McGee, ed.	*Pragmatic Bioethics.* Nashville, TN: Vanderbilt University Press, 1999.
Bill McKibben	*Enough: Staying Human in an Engineered Age.* New York: Henry Holt, 2003.
Stephen J. O'Brien	*Tears of the Cheetah and Other Tales from the Genetic Frontier.* New York: Thomas Dunne, 2003.
Gregory E. Pence	*Re-Creating Medicine: Ethical Issues at the Frontiers of Medicine.* Lanham, MD: Rowman & Littlefield, 2000.
Ted Peters	*Playing God? Genetic Determinism and Human Freedom.* New York: Routledge, 2003.
Susanna Hornig Priest	*A Grain of Truth: The Media, the Public, and Biotechnology.* Lanham, MD: Rowman & Littlefield, 2001.
Vandana Shiva	*Tomorrow's Biodiversity.* London: Thames & Hudson, 2000.
Martin Teitel and Kimberly A. Wilson, eds.	*Genetically Engineered Food: Changing the Nature of Nature.* Rochester, VT: Park Street, 1999.
Colin Tudge	*The Impact of the Gene: From Mendel's Peas to Designer Babies.* New York: Hill and Wang, 2000.
Casey Walker, ed.	*Made Not Born: The Troubling World of Biotechnology.* San Francisco: Sierra Club Books, 2000.
Raymond A. Zilinskas, ed.	*Biological Warfare: Modern Offense and Defense.* Boulder, CO: Lynn Rienner, 2000.

Periodicals

Anil Ananthaswamy	"Genetic Tinkering Turns One Species into Another," *New Scientist*, March 8, 2003.
Nell Boyce	"Engineered to Run Wild," *U.S. News & World Report*, June 3, 2002.
Business Week	"Everything You Need to Know About Cloning," April 29, 2002.
Sreeram Chaulia	"Science for Humanity or Profit?" *Social Policy*, Summer 2002.
James F. Childress	"Human Cloning and Human Dignity: The Report of the President's Council on Bioethics," *Hastings Center Report*, May/June 2003.
Christopher F. Chyba	"Toward Biological Security," *Foreign Affairs*, May/June 2002.
Marcy Darnovsky	"Embryo Cloning and Beyond," *Tikkun*, July/August 2002.

Mark Dowie   "Talking Apes, Flying Pigs, Superhumans with
                      Armadillo Attributes, and Other Strange Consider-
                      ations of Dr. Stuart Newman's Fight to Patent a
                      Human/Animal Chimera," *Mother Jones*, January/
                      February 2004.

Economist   "Reinventing Yesterday," March 29, 2003.

Carl Elliott   "The Importance of Being Human," *Hastings Center
                      Report*, November/December 2002.

Liz Else   "The Good Fight," *New Scientist*, March 15, 2003.

Gerald L. Epstein   "Bioresponsibility: Engaging the Scientific Com-
                      munity in Reducing the Biological Weapons
                      Threat," *BioScience*, May 2002.

Ruth Faden   "Spare Parts for the Rich? Everybody Seems to
                      Have a View on Embryo Research. But Stem Cell
                      Treatments Raise Moral Dilemmas That Few Have
                      Even Started to Consider," *New Scientist*, October
                      19, 2002.

Thomas Fields-Meyers "Send in the Clones: Biologist Robert Lanza Has a
                      Plan to Help Endangered Species Fight Extinc-
                      tion," *People Weekly*, September 8, 2003.

William FitzPatrick   "Surplus Embryos, Nonreproductive Cloning, and
                      the Intend/Foresee Distinction," *Hastings Center
                      Report*, May/June 2003.

Mark S. Frankel   "Inheritable Genetic Modification and a Brave
                      New World: Did Huxley Have It Wrong?" *Hastings
                      Center Report*, March/April 2003.

Francis Fukuyama   "In Defense of Nature, Human and Non-Human,"
                      World Watch, July/August 2002.

Alexandra M. Goho   "Life Made to Order: Scientists Are Taking Genetic
                      Engineering to the Extreme, Creating New
                      Genomes from Scratch. The Result Could Be Artifi-
                      cial Life Forms Designed to Churn Out Novel
                      Drugs or Turn Pollution into Energy," *Technology
                      Review*, April 2003.

Brian Halweil and   "Beyond Cloning: The Larger Agenda of Human
Dick Bell   Engineering," *World Watch*, July/August 2002.

Jennifer Hattam   "'We Are Plenty Good Enough': Bill McKibben on
                      Brash Plans to Tinker with Our Genes," *Sierra*, No-
                      vember/December 2003.

Richard Hayes   "The Science and Politics of Genetically Modified
                      Humans: Will New Genetic Technologies Be Care-
                      fully Controlled for Their Benefits—or Will They
                      Inadvertently Destroy Civil Society? Say Hello to
                      the Post-Human Ideology," *World Watch*, July/
                      August 2002.

Beatrice Trum Hunter "Biotech Animals Come to the Farm," *Consumers'
                      Research*, May 2001.

Wil S. Hylton "Who Owns This Body?" *Esquire*, June 2001.

D. Gale Johnson "Biotechnology Issues for Developing Economies," *Economic Development & Cultural Change*, October 2002.

Erika Jonietz "Choosing Our Children's Genetic Futures," *Technology Review*, February 2003.

Leon R. Kass "The Public's Stake (Biotechnology: A House Divided)," *Public Interest*, Winter 2003.

Charles Krauthammer "The Fatal Promise of Cloning: Advocates Say They Will Never Create Human Fetuses. Can We Believe Them?" *Time*, June 24, 2002.

I. Richard Manning "Eating the Genes," *Technology Review*, July 2001.

Charles Margulis "Playing with Our Food: A Massive Food Experiment Already Underway," *Earth Island Journal*, Winter 2002.

Kathleen S. Matthews "Exploring the Frontiers of the Future: 'One of the Central Challenges for the Future Is That We Don't Know What We Don't Know,'" *USA Today*, January 2002.

Jim Moran "Embryonic Stem Cell Research," *Humanist*, July/August 2003.

Neil Munro "Doctor Who? Scientists Are Treated as Objective Arbiters in the Cloning Debate. But Most Have Serious Skin in the Game," *Washington Monthly*, November 2002.

National Research Council "NRC Reports on Concerns About Animal Biotechnology," *Journal of Environmental Health*, January/February 2003.

Robert L. Paarlberg "Reinvigorating Genetically Modified Crops: Poor Farmers in Developing Nations Will Benefit if the United States Asserts Itself in the International Arena to Develop and Promote Biotechnology," *Issues in Science and Technology*, Spring 2003.

Jonathan Rauch "Will Frankenfood Save the Planet? Over the Next Half Century Genetic Engineering Could Feed Humanity and Solve a Raft of Environmental Ills—if Only Environmentalists Would Let It," *Atlantic Monthly*, October 2003.

Jeremy Rifkin "Why I Oppose Human Cloning," *Tikkun*, July/August 2002.

John Robbins "A Biological Apocalypse Averted," *Earth Island Journal*, Winter 2001.

Janet D. Rowley et al. "Harmful Moratorium on Stem Cell Research," *Science*, September 20, 2002.

M. Spriggs

"Therapeutic Cloning Research and Ethical Oversight: There Should Be Government Funding for Therapeutic Cloning Research—and Do We Really Need a Moratorium on Such Research?" *Journal of Medical Ethics*, August 2003.

Gregory Stock

"Do We Pull Back in Fear or Embrace the Future?" *Times Higher Education Supplement*, May 17, 2002.

Joni Eareckson Tada

"The Threat of Biotech: Joni Eareckson Tada Responds to Christopher Reeve and Others," *Christianity Today*, March 2003.

Time

"Future Visions: How Will Genetics Change Our Lives? TIME Invited a Panel of Scientists and Science Writers to Close Their Eyes and Imagine the World 50 Years from Now. This Is What They See," February 17, 2003.

Patrice J. Tuohy

"A Perfect Joy: Are Our Ethics Keeping Pace with the Current Genetic Revolution?" *U.S. Catholic*, June 2003.

David G. Victor and C. Ford Runge

"Farming the Genetic Frontier," *Foreign Affairs*, May/June 2002.

Adam Wolfson and Ronald Bailey

"Does Genetic Engineering Endanger Human Freedom?" *American Enterprise*, October 2001.

Wendy Wolfson

"Raising the Steaks: Fancy a Beefburger but Want to Spare the Cow? Try Growing Meat in a Lab Dish," *New Scientist*, December 21, 2002.

Index

137